HEARING GOD'S VOICE

MIKE RICHES

[jesus-ministry series]

Hearing God's Voice
Third Edition, July 2007

Published by Jesus Ministry International, a ministry of Destiny City Church, Tacoma, WA.
www.jesusministryintl.org

ISBN 978-0-9797798-1-7

JESUS MINISTRY INTERNATIONAL
PO BOX 2014
Tacoma, WA 98401
Printed in the USA

CONTENTS

PREFACE

Why did I decide to write this book? Good question. I certainly do not consider myself to be an expert on this subject. Others much more qualified have written well on the topic of hearing the voice of God. I highly recommend the books written by Dr. Wayne Grudem and Dr. Jack Deere along with many others, for more technical and comprehensive works on this subject. I don't take lightly the warning from King Solomon when he wrote in Ecclesiastes 12:12 (NASB) "*But beyond this, my son, be warned: the writing of many books is endless, and excessive devotion to books is wearying to the body.*" Now Solomon was certainly not on the top of his game when he wrote Ecclesiastes, but he just might have a point! So with all this in mind, why did I go ahead and write this book?

First of all, I firmly believe I was directed to do so by the Lord. Second, I simply want to share our experience and what we are learning on the amazing truth that God does speak directly to people today (yes, including you). Personally, my wife and I come from a theological heritage that does not include an understanding of God speaking directly today. In fact, our church body is from a heritage that would definitely be very skeptical of anyone saying God still speaks. Needless to say, it caused some reverberations and stirring when God showed up in our church body and shattered our prior understanding.

This book is designed to share a bit of what the Lord has taught us (as individuals and a church body) about hearing His voice. I know we have benefited much by those who have gone before us in recent church history. We have benefited both from their blunders and successes in recovering the truth of God's intimate voice. We are indebted. I read many books and articles on this subject when God began to wake us up to this reality. I never knew I would write on the subject. Like Solomon, I know that there is nothing new under the sun. What I mean is this: I am positive that very little in this booklet is original to me, except our experiences. I have spent many hours studying and reading on this subject (for survival), and I know much of what I now understand is the result of my learning from others. Unfortunately, I would be hard pressed to specifically give credit where it is due. For that I apologize in advance. Most of what you will read in this booklet has come from experience gained through hard lessons, teaching, and training.

We have used this material to train our church body and I hope it will be of some help to you.

If you have never considered that God can speak to you today in specific and intimate ways, I hope this booklet will provoke your thinking. If you are already experiencing this joy in your relationship with God; I trust that you will be encouraged and stimulated to new depths of intimacy with the Lord.

PART 1
ESTABLISHING THE TRUTH THAT GOD SPEAKS TODAY

CHAPTER 1

INTRODUCTION

INTRODUCTION: DOES GOD SPEAK TODAY?

I never had to face the question of "Does God still speak directly today" until I was in my early forties. My parents became devoted followers of Jesus Christ when I was about twelve, and our participation in a local church became very active from that time forward. By the time I was twenty-two, I began to follow the Lord with abandonment to the best of my understanding. I was almost thirty when I entered into occupational ministry as a pastor. I was a pastor for nearly fifteen years before I was forced to seriously confront this topic.

The topic became more than a theological argument when it hit my house. After fifteen years of ministry, My wife began to receive clear communiqué "from the Lord" in specific and diverse ways. Much of what she received was explicit and had immediate fulfillment in real life events.

You need to understand that my wife is a very down to earth type of person. She is not flashy or sensationalistic. She is plainspoken and rock solid in her knowledge of the Scriptures. Up to that point this was not a normal occurrence for her. And on top of that, a few others in our church began to have similar experiences. These people were all trusted and stable leaders, whom I had known for quite some time. They began to ask questions about what was taking place. I was scrambling to biblically answer them! It is interesting to consider that I had been a devoted follower of Jesus Christ and in ministry for many years, without ever seriously having to confront this issue. But the time had come.

In February 2000, I was thrown into the deep end of the pool. In fact, I felt like I was dropped out of a plane into the middle of the Pacific Ocean. God began to manifest Himself in supernatural ways, including prolifically speaking to us (There could be a whole book written on all of the "God invasion" that happened to us during that time). I had other elders and staff walk through this time with me, but I certainly felt the stress of addressing this issue under pressing circumstances (which included other manifestations of God's supernatural power, but that is a story for another time).

People within our conservative evangelical church were looking for responses, answers, and direction. During the subsequent months, many people left our church over this issue, and other issues related to

God's demonstrated power. In fact, we were accused of becoming a cult—for isn't this how Joseph Smith operated in the founding of Mormonism? Many of the folks in our congregation watched good friends and family members leave. It was a very unsettling experience for them. Previously, we had been in a pretty stable seven years of exciting growth as we grew from 170 to approximately 1500 people. This "exodus" was unusual and disquieting for our church.

My spiritual heritage is of a strong scriptural emphasis. Therefore, my default response to addressing the events around me was to immediately dig into the scripture. I began to read the Bible from cover to cover with fresh eyes, looking for every time God spoke. I also did many topical studies concerning the prophetic and God speaking. In fact, I took a brand new Bible and highlighted in yellow all the verses in which God directly spoke or in which the topic of Him speaking was addressed. I tried to read the Scriptures fresh as if I were reading them for the first time. I had to come to a personal understanding of the subject, but I also needed to lead the church in understanding as well.

The following is an overview of some of the main

themes I addressed in my studies. Again, I do not claim to be an expert on this subject. But it is my desire to share some of what the Lord has taught us as we have traveled down this faith road.

CHAPTER 2

GOD SPEAKING TO MANKIND IS THE NORM

As I began highlighting verses (in my new Bible) where God spoke to mankind, I observed that there were very few pages that were not yellow. God speaking to mankind was the norm throughout the scripture. Biblical history is filled with God to talking to His people. In fact, it is unusual when He *doesn't* speak.

THE OLD TESTAMENT

We know God communed with Adam and Eve in Eden's Garden. He talked with Cain. Noah had some interesting conversations with God, as did Abraham, Isaac, Jacob, and Joseph. What about Moses and Joshua? God even spoke during the period of the Judges, when the people of Israel continually disregarded and disobeyed God. He still spoke to people like Deborah, Gideon, Samson, and the nation of Israel through prophets. Samuel had both challenges and blessings due to hearing God's voice. How about David and Solomon? Of course, what would we expect as we read *the prophets*?

THE NEW TESTAMENT

God's voice did not go silent in the New Testament.

There is Zechariah, Mary and Joseph, along with the shepherds, the magi, Simeon, and others. The book of Acts continues to demonstrate that God loves to talk to His people; He loves it when His people seek His mind and heart. How did Peter and John know that God desired to heal the lame man at the Temple? How did Peter know that Ananias and Sapphira had hoodwinked everyone but God, and that God was going to judge them with physical death? How did the little known but godly Ananias of Acts 9 know that he was to pray healing and Holy Spirit-filling on Saul of Tarsus? How did Saul of Tarsus simultaneously know that Ananias would be coming to him?

Cornelius was shocked as God spoke to him through an angel, while God was directly speaking to His servant Peter about going to minister to a Gentile named Cornelius. God spoke to church leaders in Antioch to send out Barnabas and Paul on a mission trip. The rest of Acts is an amazing display of God communicating with His people through words, angels, the Scriptures, impressions on the inner man, visions, and people with prophetic gifting.

The New Testament epistles then describe the gifts related to God speaking to people and how they are to be employed. We also read how God imparted gifting to people through prophetic words; such as the gifts Timothy received.

> **1 Timothy 4:14 (NLT)** Do not neglect the spiritual gift you received through the prophecies spoken to you when the elders of the church laid their hands on you.

> **2 Timothy 1:6 (NLT)** This is why I remind you to fan into flames the spiritual gift God gave you when I laid my hands on you.

We certainly cannot ignore the direction that Timothy received regarding his ministry. They came directly from prophetic words spoken over him.

> **1 Timothy 1:18 (NLT)** Timothy, my son, here are my instructions for you, based on the prophetic words spoken about you earlier. May they give you the confidence to fight well in the Lord's battles.

Of course, what needs to be said about the Apocalypse, the book of Revelation? It is an amazing demonstration of God speaking to mankind in an exceptional manner.

There are so many other individuals to whom God spoke throughout the Scriptures. They were all manner of people with diverse backgrounds. They included kings, priests, and prophets as well as farmers, shepherds, moms and dads, and unassuming business people. The Scriptures present an exciting kaleidoscope of God speaking to mankind in powerful ways. Put yourself in Moses' sandals. A bush starts to burn but won't burn up. Then, if that weren't strange enough, God *speaks* through the bush! What was it like for Daniel when an angel approached him, or Joseph, Mary, and the shepherds? Or how do you prepare dinner for the angel of the Lord like Abraham did? What would you do after waking up from a trance (like Peter) realizing that God had spoke to you? The Scriptures are anything but dull when it comes to God speaking to His people!

THE REST OF CHURCH HISTORY

Through my casual reading of biographies through the years, I have read many church history accounts. God has spoken to many great men and women of the faith. I have not thoroughly researched the subject, but I recommend that you read Jack Deere's book titled "Surprised by the Voice of God."[1] There is a section in his book where he follows the course of church history with documentation of saints to whom God specifically spoke.

WHEN GOD DOESN'T SPEAK, IT IS NOT A GOOD SIGN

In my reading and studying of Scripture, I did note times in which God did not readily speak to His people. These were times of sin and reprobation, times of unbelief and rebellion. It seemed to be an indication of God's judgment upon His people when He rarely spoke.

During the time of the Judges, God did speak (as I mentioned earlier) but it was not common as noted in First Samuel chapter one. We read that when God began speaking to Samuel, he did not discern it was the Lord and neither did the priest Eli. During that time period, it was uncommon to receive a word from the Lord.

> **1 Samuel 3:1 (NASB)** Now the boy Samuel was ministering to the LORD before Eli. And word from the LORD was rare in those days, visions were infrequent.

The spiritual climate of Israel during this period of time is described for us in the last verse of Judges.

> **Judges 21:25 (NASB)** In those days there was no king in Israel; everyone did what was right in his own eyes.

This is an appropriate description of the entire four hundred year period of the judges except for brief periods of repentance that led to intermittent revivals. We repeatedly read of Israel's reprobate ways.

> **Judges 3:7 (NLT)** The Israelites did what was evil in the LORD's sight. They forgot about the LORD their God, and they worshiped the images of Baal and the Asherah poles.

> **Judges 3:12 (NLT)** Once again the Israelites did what was evil in the LORD's sight, so the LORD gave King Eglon of Moab control over Israel.

> **Judges 4:1 (NLT)** After Ehud's death, the Israelites again did what was evil in the LORD's sight.

You get the picture. This continues throughout the book of Judges. During this time, words from the Lord were rare. It was because Israel was not spiritually healthy.

Reading through the Scriptures, it was easy to see that God not only loves to speak to His people, but that He wants us to inquire of Him. He desires us to ask Him questions, actually expecting that He will answer. He wants to speak to the most intimate details of our lives. In fact, I noticed several verses that revealed God's judgment against His people for not inquiring of Him.

> **Zephaniah 1:4-6 (NASB)** "So I will stretch out My hand against Judah And against all the inhabitants of Jerusalem. And I will cut off the remnant of Baal from this place, *And* the names of the idolatrous priests along with the priests. And those who bow down on the housetops to the host of heaven, And those who bow down *and* swear to the LORD and *yet* swear by Milcom [Molech], And those who have turned back from following the LORD, And those who have not sought the LORD or inquired of Him."

When you read the above verses in Zephaniah you note that there are some pretty vile sins mentioned; from demonic idolatry to embracing a religion that sacrificed children. In this vile list is included "not seeking or inquiring of the Lord." It is fairly easy to see that the Lord takes our communication with Him seriously. God didn't just speak during a special season of history, speaking is the norm. We are to be very concerned when God is not speaking, for it is likely a sign of God's displeasure.

GOD SPEAKS IN DIVERSE WAYS TO DIVERSE SUBJECTS IN THE OLD TESTAMENT

The Scriptures are filled with God speaking to His people and His people inquiring of Him. Such Scriptures are so abundant that I cannot list them all, but below are a few good examples. Note the spectrum of topics that God freely spoke to; from "big picture" issues to seemingly minor details.

> **1 Samuel 23:1-6 (NLT)** One day news came to David that the Philistines were at Keilah stealing grain from the threshing floors. David asked the LORD, "Should I go and attack them?" "Yes, go and save Keilah," the LORD told him. But David's men said, "We're afraid even here in Judah. We certainly don't want to go to Keilah to fight the whole Philistine army!" So David asked the LORD again, and again the LORD replied, "Go down to Keilah, for I will help you conquer the Philistines." So David and his men went to Keilah. They slaughtered the Philistines and took all their livestock and rescued the people of Keilah. Abiathar the priest went to Keilah with David, taking the ephod with him to get answers for David from the LORD.

> **1 Samuel 23: 9-12 (NLT)** But David learned of Saul's plan and told Abiathar the priest to bring the ephod and ask the LORD what he should do. And David prayed, "O LORD, God of Israel, I have heard that Saul is planning to come and destroy Keilah because I

am here. Will the men of Keilah surrender me to him? And will Saul actually come as I have heard? O LORD, God of Israel, please tell me." And the LORD said, "He will come." Again David asked, "Will these men of Keilah really betray me and my men to Saul?" And the LORD replied, "Yes, they will betray you."

1 Samuel 30:8 (NLT) Then David asked the LORD, "Should I chase them? Will I catch them?" And the LORD told him, "Yes, go after them. You will surely recover everything that was taken from you!"

2 Samuel 2:1 (NLT) After this, David asked the LORD, "Should I move back to Judah?" And the LORD replied, "Yes." Then David asked, "Which town should I go to?" And the LORD replied "Hebron."

2 Samuel 5:19, 23-25 (NLT) So David asked the LORD, "Should I go out to fight the Philistines? Will You hand them over to me?" The LORD replied, "Yes, go ahead. I will certainly give you the victory." And once again David asked the LORD what to do. "Do not attack them straight on," the LORD replied. "Instead, circle around behind them and attack them near the balsam trees. When you hear a sound like marching feet in the tops of the balsam trees, attack! That will be the signal that the LORD is moving ahead of you to strike down the Philistines." So David did what the LORD commanded, and he struck down the Philistines all the way from Gibeon to Gezer.

1 Kings 3:5 (NLT) That night the LORD appeared to Solomon in a dream, and God said, "What do you want? Ask, and I will give it to you!"

Nehemiah 2:12, 7:5 (NLT) I slipped out during the night, taking only a few others with me. I had not told anyone about the plans God had put in my heart for Jerusalem. We took no pack animals with us, except the donkey that I myself was riding . . . So my God gave me the idea to call together all the leaders of the city, along with the ordinary citizens, for registration.

We read in the preceding verses that God spoke to King David as to whether he should take his nation to war. We also read that God gave David, Joshua and others war strategies. He also spoke to whether or not David should move his residence, including identifying the town which would become David's new residence. God declared a life-characterizing blessing and established a life-covenant with King Solomon through a dream. The plans for restoring a city, Jerusalem, were given to Nehemiah. The issues were diverse. God wants us to seek His mind and follow His specific will. It is arrogance on our part to do otherwise.

GOD SPEAKS TO HIS PEOPLE IN THE NEW TESTAMENT TO DIRECT AND STRENGTHEN

Several verses in the book of Acts demonstrate how God directed His people, as well as His Church and her development, by speaking directly. As you read the following Scriptures from the book of Acts, I think that it is important to remember that in recorded Scripture we do not have every historical incident of every person's life. I believe we can safely assume that there were many other individuals God spoke to and through. He did so to direct, comfort, warn, and strengthen His people.

> **Acts 8:26 (NLT)** As for Philip, an angel of the Lord said to him, "Go south down the desert road that runs from Jerusalem to Gaza."

> **Acts 9:10-12 (NLT)** Now there was a believer in Damascus named Ananias. The Lord spoke to him in a vision, calling, "Ananias! "Yes, Lord!" he replied. The Lord said, "Go over to Straight Street, to the house of Judas. When you arrive, ask for Saul of Tarsus. He is praying to me right now. I have shown him a vision of a man named Ananias coming in and laying his hands on him so that he can see again."

> **Acts 10:3-4, 9-10 (NLT)** One afternoon about three o'clock, he had a vision in which he saw an angel of

God coming toward him. "Cornelius!" the angel said. Cornelius stared at him in terror. "What is it, sir?" he asked the angel. And the angel replied, "Your prayers and gifts to the poor have not gone unnoticed by God. . . " The next day as Cornelius's messengers were nearing the city, Peter went up to the flat roof to pray. It was about noon, and he was hungry. But while lunch was being prepared, he fell into a trance.

Acts 13:2-3 (NLT) One day as these men were worshiping the Lord and fasting, the Holy Spirit said, "Dedicate Barnabas and Saul for the special work I have for them." So after more fasting and prayer, the men laid their hands on them and sent them on their way.

Acts 15:32 (NLT) Then Judas and Silas, both being prophets, spoke extensively to the Christians, encouraging and strengthening their faith.

Acts 16:9-10 (NLT) That night Paul had a vision. He saw a man from Macedonia in northern Greece, pleading with him, "Come over here and help us." So we decided to leave for Macedonia at once, for we could only conclude that God was calling us to preach the Good News there.

Acts 16:16-18 (NLT) One day as we were going down to the place of prayer, we met a demon-possessed slave girl. She was a fortune-teller who earned a lot of money for her masters.She followed along behind us shouting, "These men are servants of the Most High God, and they have come to tell you how to be saved." This went on day after day until Paul got so exasperated that he turned and spoke to the demon within her. "I command you in the name of Jesus Christ to come out of her," he said. And instantly it left her.

Acts 18:9-10 (NLT) One night the Lord spoke to Paul in a vision and told him, "Don't be afraid! Speak out! Don't be silent! For I am with you, and no one will harm you because many people here in this city belong to me."

Acts 20:22-24 (NLT) "And now I am going to Jerusalem, drawn there irresistibly by the Holy Spirit, not knowing what awaits me, except that the Holy Spirit has told me in city after city that jail and suffering lie ahead. But my life is worth nothing unless I use it for doing the work assigned me by the Lord Jesus--the work of telling others the Good News about God's wonderful kindness and love. "

Acts 21:4, 8-9 (NLT) We went ashore, found the local believers, and stayed with them a week. These disciples prophesied through the Holy Spirit that Paul should not go on to Jerusalem. . . . Then we went on to Caesarea and stayed at the home of Philip the Evangelist, one of the seven men who had been chosen to distribute food. He had four unmarried daughters who had the gift of prophecy.

Acts 21:10-14 (NLT) During our stay of several days, a man named Agabus, who also had the gift of prophecy, arrived from Judea. When he visited us, he took Paul's belt and bound his own feet and hands with it. Then he said, "The Holy Spirit declares, `So shall the owner of this belt be bound by the Jewish leaders in Jerusalem and turned over to the Romans.'" When we heard this, we who were traveling with him, as well as the local believers, begged Paul not to go on to Jerusalem. But he said, "Why all this weeping? You are breaking my heart! For I am ready not only to be jailed at Jerusalem but also to die for the sake of the Lord Jesus." When it was clear that we couldn't persuade him, we gave up and said, "The will of the Lord be done."

Acts 27:21-26 (NLT) No one had eaten for a long time. Finally, Paul called the crew together and said, "Men, you should have listened to me in the first place and not left Fair Havens. You would have avoided all this injury and loss. But take courage! None of you will lose your lives, even though the ship will go down. For last night an angel of the God to whom I belong and whom I serve stood beside me, and he said, `Don't be afraid, Paul, for you will surely stand trial before Caesar! What's more, God in his goodness has granted safety to everyone sailing with you.' So take courage! For I believe God. It will be just as He said."

Ministry direction was given to Philip while Ananias received a specific call of ministry for Saul of Tarsus. God wanted it to be made clear that salvation was for the gentiles as well, so He prepared the heart of Cornelius, and the missionary Peter, through diverse and dramatic communication. Through prophetic direction, Church leaders sent out a missionary team that would change the world. Prophets were used to bless and encourage the Church. Paul was able to look past a servant-girl's right-sounding words to find demonic opposition. The Apostle Paul received the explicit geographical direction where his missionary work was to proceed. Encouragement, direction, and strength were continuously realized via God speaking specifically to His people throughout the book of Acts.

SUMMARY

Does God desire to speak to His people? Absolutely. Is God serious about us inquiring of Him, and listening to Him? Absolutely. God desires to direct us, protect us, and provide for us through his intimate voice today. I am convinced that we would operate more strategically, efficiently, and with more power if we would learn to go to the Lord and listen to Him. Think of the possibilities! God actually wants to talk with us. He actually wants to direct us. We are literally sitting on a powder keg!

There is much skepticism and legitimate concern surrounding this subject. Some skepticism is well deserved, while some is simply unfounded. People have been manipulated and injured by those who have misrepresented this amazing treasure of God. Some are skeptical because they essentially do not believe that God still speaks as He did in Scripture. I want to briefly address this skepticism and some of the contributing factors.

With respect to those who believe that God no longer speaks as He did in the Scriptures, my response is two-fold. First, I cannot objectively find any legitimate Scriptural basis for such a position; even though I am certainly predisposed, sympathetic, and vulnerable to such a position due to my spiritual heritage and prior experience. Really, I simply cannot find biblical backing for the position. Second, and subordinate to my first response, is that my experience in these recent years says otherwise. This is not relegated merely to my personal experience or that of my wife, but to the credible experience of hundreds of others in our church and other believers we are meeting from around the world. The stories are seemingly endless and mind-boggling! God wants to intricately interface with your life as He did with biblical personalities. The joy is indescribable!

The infinite Creator of this universe, the transcendent and eternal God, desires to communicate personally and intimately with you and me. He wants to speak to us specifically for He delights in every detail of our lives. The Scriptures must always be paramount to us just as they were for King David and the apostles Peter and Paul. *Everything must be measured by Scripture*, as it must be our sole basis for faith (doctrine) and practice. But I do not believe God's design was to speak only through the Scriptures.

As was mentioned earlier, some of the skepticism concerning this topic is well deserved. It is true, many people and ministries have been hurt because of the abuse of this spiritual blessing, grace, gift, and discipline. As a result, this truth has been discredited and denied legitimacy. The Scriptures give an abundance of safeguards to protect us. We must understand and apply these safeguards. But, I also think there is much debate over this topic for anther reason—Satan does not want us to hear God's voice!

If the Church truly believed, cherished, safeguarded, and competently walked in hearing God's voice; what affect would it have on the Church? I believe it would be powerful! How did hearing God's voice benefit Moses in his dealings with Pharaoh? How about Joshua and Gideon in their battles, or King David in building the nation of Israel into a world power? How did hearing God's voice benefit Peter, Paul, and the early Church as Jesus' ministry and kingdom was strategically advanced?

As we understand that our one world is comprised of two realms, one spiritual and the other physical, the playing field is leveled when we seek the Lord. He knows what is going on! Remember, we do not wrestle against flesh and blood, but against spirit beings in the spiritual realm (I suggest our booklet on this subject, "One World – Two Realms: Operating in Christ's Authority").

If you were Satan, would you want the Church to use this tool? *Hell trembles at the thought.* He must discredit this weapon and thereby severely disadvantage the Church. He can't afford you as an individual, or

God's people corporately, to authentically move in this divine asset. Can you imagine being given insight regarding the spiritual world and specific decisions you must make in life? You and I, and the Church corporately, need to recover this heavenly resource. Hearing God's voice is not to be relegated to the wild-eyed, crazy haired eccentrics, but to every single one of us. Let's look at some foundational truths in understanding and walking in "Hearing God's Voice."

CHAPTER 3

GOD IS SPEAKING; ARE WE LISTENING?

God does speak, and He speaks right to the context of "real-time" situations. God is a communicating God; but the question is, "Do we hear, identify, and understand His voice?" God speaks to His children in the normal course of our lives. Hearing God is to be the heartbeat of Church life and ministry. I believe that God speaks regularly to you and me; but we simply are not sensitive and attuned to His voice. I am reminded of Samuel, a young man serving the priest Eli.

> **1 Samuel 3:1-13 (NLT)** Meanwhile, the boy Samuel was serving the LORD by assisting Eli. Now in those days messages from the LORD were very rare, and visions were quite uncommon. One night Eli, who was almost blind by now, had just gone to bed. The lamp of God had not yet gone out, and Samuel was sleeping in the Tabernacle near the Ark of God. Suddenly, the LORD called out, "Samuel! Samuel!" "Yes?" Samuel replied. "What is it?" He jumped up and ran to Eli. "Here I am. What do you need?" "I didn't call you," Eli replied. "Go on back to bed." So he did. Then the LORD called out again, "Samuel!" Again Samuel jumped up and ran to Eli. "Here I am," he said. "What do you need?" "I didn't call you, my son," Eli said. "Go on back to bed." Samuel did not yet know the LORD because he had never had a message from the LORD before. So now the LORD called a third time, and once more Samuel jumped up and ran to Eli. "Here I

> am," he said. "What do you need?" Then Eli realized it was the LORD who was calling the boy. So he said to Samuel, "Go and lie down again, and if someone calls again, say, 'Yes, LORD, your servant is listening.' " So Samuel went back to bed. And the LORD came and called as before, "Samuel! Samuel!" And Samuel replied, "Yes, your servant is listening." Then the LORD said to Samuel, "I am about to do a shocking thing in Israel. I am going to carry out all my threats against Eli and his family. I have warned him continually that judgment is coming for his family, because his sons are blaspheming God and he hasn't disciplined them."

God was speaking to Samuel, but Samuel was not familiar with God's voice. Apparently, neither was Eli, the priest. This is similar to many of us who are God's children. I have many Samuel-like stories I can personally share with you, but let me share just one.

When I was almost thirty years old, my wife and I believed the Lord was directing us to enter occupational ministry. I quit my job, we sold our home, our new automobiles, and most all of our possessions to downsize for a life of ministry. We prepared to move three hundred miles away to plant a church. We needed to buy a good "pre-owned" car that we could purchase with cash. It needed to be a car that would be pretty much maintenance free, because our future finances were a mystery at that point.

We determined to get up on a Saturday morning to go car shopping. My wife woke up and told me she had a dream the night before. In the dream she saw us walking up to a blue sedan that was a General Motors make, which we purchased. She then went on to say that she believed the Lord was going to give us a blue car to purchase. This did not sit well at all with me. First of all the task of kicking tires, looking under car hoods, listening to engines, feeling for the shifting of transmissions, and purchasing a car was a "guy-thing." Second, her little story sounded a bit mystical to me. Since when did we make decisions based on dreams? And besides, why would God be concerned about a car purchase? There were much bigger issues in the world to attend to — right? Let's simply use our common sense and wisdom. Besides, what was I going to tell my friends, "*We purchased a new car by driving up and down 'auto-row' looking for a blue car that my wife saw in a dream?*"

Of course, I did not say all of that to my wife (give me some credit for wisdom and leadership aptitude), we simply went shopping. I drove down to the "auto-row" in our little town, into the first dealership we came to and proceeded directly to the "pre-owned" car section (back then they called them "used" cars, a rather undignified term). As I drove onto the lot, I noticed directly to my left, two rows off the street a blue sedan, General Motors make. I drove by it as quickly as I could; pretending I did not notice it - but my wife spotted it immediately. She said, "That was the car I saw in my dream last night." This was way too spooky for me. I replied that we had to be wise and look the lot over and proceeded to get as far away from that blue sedan as possible. I accomplished my objective and asked my wife if she was going to get out and test-drive some cars. She replied by saying there was no need to until we test drove the blue sedan.

I was determined to find any other car. At the end of the day, after I had lost count of the cars I had driven that simply were not acceptable, I returned to the lot with the blue car. We test drove that car (yes "we" test drove that car), and after swallowing my pride, we made the purchase. We ended up driving that car for years and never did more than change the oil. We took it to get serviced; but there was simply never anything wrong with it. I called it the "wilderness wanderings car" because its parts never wore out and its tires never blistered. There was no doubt that God had spoken to us through my wife's dream, to direct us in the detail of purchasing our car. But I, like Samuel, was unfamiliar with God's manner of speaking.

CHAPTER 4

DEFINITIONS

It is important for us to define what we mean by "hearing God's voice." This booklet is not designed to be academically technical, but to be readable and accessible to every believing follower of Jesus Christ. We must give definition to certain terms to clarify meaning. Terms such as "prophecy," "prophetic disclosure," "subjective revelation," or "words of knowledge" are used to communicate a spontaneous communication from God to mankind other than the Scriptures (which is called "special revelation"). The following are a few definitions and commentaries regarding the term "prophesy." We begin with a simplified definition of the Greek word "propheteuo" from *Strong's Concordance.*

> Strong's Concordance: It means to prophesy, to be a prophet, speak forth by divine inspirations, to predict, to prophesy with the idea of foretelling future events pertaining especially to the kingdom of God, to utter forth, declare a thing which can only be known by divine revelation, to break forth under sudden impulse in lofty discourse or praise of the divine counsels, under like prompting, to teach, refute, reprove, admonish, comfort others, to act as a prophet, discharge the prophetic office.[1]

> Wayne Grudem: Although several definitions have been given for the gift of prophecy, a fresh examination of the New Testament teaching on this gift will show

that it should be defined not as "predicting the future," nor as proclaiming a word from the Lord," nor as "powerful preaching"—but rather as "*telling something that God has brought to mind.*"[3]

Fredrick Dale Bruner: ". . . prophecy is felt to be spontaneous and direct spiritual communication, it is not to be confused with preaching or prepared remarks where the substance is obtained by more conventional or indirect means than immediate inspiration. The Spirit delivers His mind and heart spontaneously and directly to the assembly through His prophets."[4]

I personally like to use the following working definition for the term prophecy;

"A supernatural ability that God gives to believers to receive a message disclosed by Him. This primarily (but not exclusively) is an immediate or spontaneous message that is communicated in diverse manners."

Larry D. Hart expands on any definition regarding the prophetic or God's subjective revelation to mankind when he states;

"It should be emphasized that the type of revelation referred to here is clearly subordinate to Scripture. In fact, the primary way in which the Spirit communicates to us is through the Bible. All other perceived

> communications from Him should be gauged by Scripture and by the spiritual discernment of seasoned saints." [5]

Hart continues by quoting J. Rodman Williams:

> "There is *nothing more to be added* [to special revelation, the Scriptures]: God's truth has been fully declared. Accordingly, what occurs in revelation within the Christian community is not new truth that goes beyond the special revelation (if so, it is spurious and not of God). It is only a deeper appreciation of what has already been revealed, or a disclosure of what has already been revealed, or a disclosure of some message for the contemporary situation that adds nothing essentially to what He has before made known." [6]

For the purpose of this book I do not want us to get caught up in terminology, but simply to understand that God speaks today to His people. I will interchangeably use the terms "prophetic," "prophetic disclosure," "revelatory disclosure" and "hearing God's voice." Certain terms carry a lot of baggage in understanding and emotion in the church. I want to demystify the terminology. Jesus declared in simple and no uncertain terms that His sheep hear His voice! Some are specifically gifted at hearing God's voice, but all of God's children can hear God speak. It really is my heart cry to make these truths usable for all of us!

CHAPTER 5

IT WAS PROMISED FOR GOD'S PEOPLE LIVING IN THIS TIME

On the Jewish holiday Pentecost, fifty days following Jesus Christ's resurrection, God manifested His presence in a powerful way. He fulfilled His promise to the apostles and early disciples by sending the Holy Spirit to them. In Acts 2 we read that one hundred twenty disciples instantaneously began speaking in languages from around the world. These were languages that they had not formally studied, but through the Holy Spirit this supernatural capacity was given. The large crowd that had gathered in Jerusalem (from diverse lands with diverse languages) was simply amazed!

To quiet the false assumptions and accusations from the crowd as to what was taking place (such as the disciples being drunk at 9:00 am), Peter shared this occurrence was the fulfillment of biblical prophecy. He began his explanation by referring to a prophecy in Joel 2 saying;

> **Acts 2:17-18 (NLT)** "In the last days," God said, "I will pour out My Spirit upon all people. Your sons and daughters will prophesy, your young men will see visions, and your old men will dream dreams. In those days I will pour out My Spirit upon all my servants, men and women alike, and they will prophesy."

He was telling the people that they were witnessing the beginning of the last days, which would be characterized by people prophesying. Sons and daughters would prophesy while young men would see visions and old men would dream dreams. For when this day arrived, God would pour out His Spirit on all of His servants, men and women alike, and they would prophesy.

What was significant about this is that people in the Old Testament who were anointed or filled by God's Holy Spirit would prophesy. This Jewish audience certainly would be familiar with this evidence of Holy Spirit infilling. This is vividly demonstrated regarding the leaders who were to assist Moses in Numbers chapter eleven.

> **Numbers 11:25-29 (NLT)** And the LORD came down in the cloud and spoke to Moses. He took some of the Spirit that was upon Moses and put it upon the seventy leaders. They prophesied as the Spirit rested upon them, but that was the only time this happened. Two men, Eldad and Medad, were still in the camp when the Spirit rested upon them. They were listed among the leaders but had not gone out to the Tabernacle, so they prophesied there in the camp. A young man ran and reported to Moses, "Eldad and Medad are prophesying in the camp!" Joshua son of Nun, who had been Moses' personal assistant since his youth,

> protested, "Moses, my master, make them stop!" But Moses replied, "Are you jealous for my sake? I wish that all the LORD's people were prophets, and that the LORD would put his Spirit upon them all!"

Another Old Testament example of this is evidenced when King Saul is anointed to be Israel's first king by Samuel.

> **1 Samuel 10:1; 5-6; 10 (NLT)** Then Samuel took a flask of olive oil and poured it over Saul's head. He kissed Saul on the cheek and said, "I am doing this because the LORD has appointed you to be the leader of his people Israel. . . "When you arrive at Gibeah of God, where the garrison of the Philistines is located, you will meet a band of prophets coming down from the altar on the hill. They will be playing a harp, a tambourine, a flute, and a lyre, and they will be prophesying. At that time the Spirit of the LORD will come upon you with power, and you will prophesy with them. You will be changed into a different person. . . " When Saul and his servant arrived at Gibeah, they saw the prophets coming toward them. Then the Spirit of God came upon Saul, and he, too, began to prophesy.

Such filling of God's Spirit was given to individuals in the Old Testament to fulfill specific tasks or functions. Such anointing would be reserved mostly for kings, queens, priests, and prophets; for it was not common to all mankind in the Old Testament.

In his Pentecost explanation, Peter was saying that one of the marks of the arrival of the "last days" was the release of God's Spirit upon all God's people. This included servants, young people, men and women. Since one of the classic evidences of Holy Spirit impartation was prophesying, then it would be reasonable that God would use such a demonstration of prophetic ministry to "usher in" this new era.

We are living in the days of the outpouring of God's Spirit. God's Spirit enables all of us to hear God's voice. We see from Joel's prophecy that this can come in different forms; from visions and dreams, to simply receiving God's prophetic words. Sometimes we like to complicate the process of hearing God's voice, but Jesus simply said that His sheep hear His voice. If you are a sheep (a follower of Christ), then you recognize His voice!

CHAPTER 6

ALL HEAR GOD'S VOICE, BUT NOT TO THE SAME DEGREE

A "SPIRITUAL GIFT" VERSUS A "CHRISTIAN GRACE"

Something that became evident as our church family began to move in hearing God's voice was that some people heard from the Lord in more significant measures than others. This became evident by the varying degrees of ease in which people received prophetic disclosure, the detail of the revelation, and the accuracy of what was received. This caused me concern from a leadership perspective on a couple of fronts.

If we truly believe that God's sheep hear His voice, then how could we keep those who did not hear God's voice as prolifically as others from shutting down? Would they be discouraged and give up? How were we going to stay on top of spiritual elitism and the divisiveness that typically surrounds this issue? How could we keep from being the "haves" and the "have nots?"

First of all, we needed to address spiritual and biblical character issues. We reminded our people that all spiritual gifts are significant in the body of Christ, the Church. Simply, we focused on keeping "servant-hood" as a preeminent virtue in the church. We also continued to cultivate and intentionally nourish the principles of "team" and "unity." In dealing with issues of spiritual gifting, there is always a battle for unity. Even the disciples argued about who would be the greatest in the kingdom! So it is a battle, but do not be discouraged, the blessing of God's voice being released far outweighs any struggle.

Second, an understanding of truth authentically released us to exhort everyone to cultivate "hearing God's voice" in their lives. I need to begin by defining a couple of terms. The terms I want to distinguish are "Christian grace" and "spiritual gift." The Greek word *charis* is many times translated by the English word "grace" such as is found in Ephesians chapter two verse eight. The Greek word *charisma* is many times translated by the English word "gift" as is the case in 1 Corinthians 12:4 with the implied word "spiritual" preceding the word "gift."

When I use the term "Christian grace" I mean the Christ-like virtues that every Christian is to cultivate. All of us are to cultivate a "servant's heart" as directed in Philippians 2:5; for that is Christ's character. We are all to grow in mercy, which is a command. Giving is to characterize the Christian and we are to become increasingly generous with our life and possessions; it is a command, not an option. We are to progressively mature in all the Christian graces, no one is exempt. Do a study on all the "one another" commands of the New Testament; there are over fifty.

"Spiritual gifts" on the other hand are particular God-given capacities administered to believers by God's grace through His Holy Spirit. These gifts supernaturally enable the believer to carry out ministry to advance God's kingdom. The following are a few helpful definitions for "spiritual gifts."

> Wayne Grudem: A spiritual gift is any ability that is empowered by the Holy Spirit and is used in ministry of the church.[7]

> Paul Enns: "Grace gifts" are sovereignly given to believers by the Holy Spirit at the moment of salvation as a special ability for service to God and to others, particularly believers.[8]

> Ray Steadman: . . . a capacity for service which is given to every true Christian without exception and which was something each did not possess before he became a Christian.[9]

No single Christian receives each and every spiritual gift, but we all receive one or more spiritual gifts by which God ministers through us. There are several lists of spiritual gifts found in the New Testament such as in 1 Corinthians 12, Romans 12, and Ephesians chapter four.

THE EXHORTATION

Every believer is to cultivate and grow in every "Christian grace" such as giving, mercy, serving, et cetera. But to each Christian is given a "spiritual gift(s)" in which they more prolifically minister. For example, I am to cultivate the Christian grace of being a merciful man. But I do not have the spiritual gift of mercy. There are people with the spiritual gift of mercy that amaze me! The power of God displayed through their acts of mercy is dynamic and life giving. Lives are changed through the actions and prayers of those gifted with mercy. They demonstrate and minister mercy like fish swim and birds fly. But just because mercy might not be my spiritual gift, I am not released from growing in, cultivating, and ministering compassion and mercy toward others.

Likewise, all of us are to cultivate the Christian

grace of hearing God speak; for the Lord's sheep hear His voice. There is no exception to this reality. But some are going to have spiritual gifts that enable them to hear God voice more prolifically and accurately. I do not have a "prophetic spiritual gift" as my wife does. But I still hear God speak, and I must work at cultivating my ability to hear God communicate to me. My wife (and others like her) seem to move much more easily and prolifically in the arena of the prophetic. What they hear is more specific, the accuracy level is higher, and what they receive is more detailed. Such individuals also have an increased responsibility to steward this gift they have been given, just like all of us must steward our spiritual gifts.

Therefore, we exhort all of our people that even though they may not be prophetically gifted, they still must understand the ways in which God speaks. Everyone must understand and apply the biblical truths and principles that help us identify God's voice. We all must work at posturing ourselves to be more sensitive to hearing God. It is an exciting reality - all believers are graced to hear God's voice!

CHAPTER 7

DO NOT DESPISE THE PROPHETIC

THREE COMMANDS

When we understand the Scriptures, we know we do not have a choice to disregard the prophetic. We are under a mandate by God. This is not an option for us, we must take it seriously. This is spelled out concisely in First Thessalonians chapter five.

> **1 Thessalonians 5:19-21 (NASB)** Do not quench the Spirit; do not despise prophetic utterances. But examine everything *carefully;* hold fast to that which is good;

There are three commands in these three verses that we must seriously consider.

COMMAND NUMBER ONE

The first command is: "do not quench the Spirit." This command says we are not to stifle God's Spirit, nor extinguish His working or movement. God's Spirit is dynamic and always moving. God is continually leading, directing, protecting, warning, convicting, comforting, and counseling His people. God's power is released to and through us by the Holy Spirit. We must not hinder His work in or through our lives.

COMMAND NUMBER TWO

It is interesting that the second command is "do not despise prophetic utterances." This command centers on not having contempt toward prophetic words or communications from the Lord. The word translated "despise" communicates considering something to be worthless, inferior, or undeserving of respect. One version translates this verse that we are not to "scoff" at prophecies. Let me take the liberty to add the word "disregard." I personally was guilty of simply disregarding the prophetic. I was guilty of giving little attention to the fact that God wanted to speak to me, my family, my friends, and/or our ministry.

When we consider the first command juxtaposed to the second, I believe it is safe to conclude that to despise prophetic utterances is to quench God's Spirit. God's Spirit moves, guides, leads, warns, and communicates God's mind and heart. He speaks in very relevant terms to God's people through the prophetic. God *loves* to speak to His people.

This again is a command. When we despise prophetic communication—it is sin! It is opposing God! We are quenching the Holy Spirit by hindering His ministry. He is trying to relay important relevant messages to us, and we are denying Him. There is no other way to put it! We have no option; we must value God speaking to us! Remember Zephaniah 1:4 states one of the reasons God judged Israel was because she no longer inquired of the Lord!

COMMAND NUMBER THREE

We are to examine carefully everything that is received and hang on to what is good. This command says we are to examine and test everything received, to see if it is of the Lord. After it has been carefully examined, we are to hold on to what is good. This is the safeguard to protect from deception and manipulation. One of the reasons that the prophetic has been discredited is because the biblical mandate to examine everything carefully has been ignored. People and ministries have been manipulated and damaged as a result.

THE REST OF THIS BOOK

The rest of this book will identify the "whys" and "ways" of God speaking to us. We will address the principles used to help us "carefully examine" what is received to determine whether or not it is of the Lord. We will also seek to understand how to protect ourselves from being deceived as we seek hearing the Lord.

PART 2
PRACTICAL IMPLEMENTATION AND APPLICATION

CHAPTER 8

THE PURPOSE OF GOD SPEAKING TO US

I am sure these are not the only purposes for which God speaks. There are other purposes found in Scripture and delineated by others on the subject. But the purposes I mention should be a good starting place in thinking about the strategic nature of the prophetic in our lives and in the Church of Jesus Christ.

PURPOSE NUMBER ONE:

To Encourage, Comfort, and Strengthen

> **1 Corinthians 14:3 (NKJV)** But he who prophesies speaks edification and exhortation and comfort to men.

It is important for God's people be strengthened, encouraged, and comforted. We need to be ministered to in this manner for we are in a war that is relentless. Satan is not out to merely make us uncomfortable, but to destroy us. The more serious we are about being significant for God and His kingdom, the more ferocious the assault. People encourage us, strengthen us, and comfort us, but sometimes God desires to speak words of encouragement directly to us.

Joshua certainly needed and received this ministry at a critical time in his life. Moses had just died. The mantel of leading the nation Israel was laid upon Joshua. The forty years of the wilderness wanderings had come to an end. Now it was time to go into the "Promised Land" and expel the inhabitants. It would be a series of mighty battles. It was going to require great faith and great courage (such as marching around massive city walls for seven days and believing that with a mere shout the walls would collapse). That is the context in which God comes to Joshua and says;

> **Joshua 1:6; 7; 9 (NLT)** "Be strong and courageous, for you will lead My people to possess all the land I swore to give their ancestors. Be strong and very courageous. Obey all the laws Moses gave you. Do not turn away from them, and you will be successful in everything you do. . . . I command you - be strong and courageous! Do not be afraid or discouraged. For the LORD your God is with you wherever you go."

I have experienced many such words spoken to me. I cannot explain how deeply the Lord has shown His love for me in this manner. One time stands out distinctly in my mind. Our church, leadership, and I personally, went through some very challenging times during the years of 2000 through 2003. God was revealing himself, and realigning our understanding of

His mission for His Church. He began to open our eyes to the dynamics of His ministry. God threw us in the deep end of the pool regarding His supernatural working and power. It was very unsettling for most of our people, and close to seventy-five percent of the people that were with us in January 2000 were no longer with us three and one-half years later. This season was very challenging and exhausting.

In the midst of this challenging season, I was in the depths of discouragement and fatigue spiritually, mentally, emotionally, and physically. I worked hard at not allowing the people to see this discouragement and fatigue in me. There are times when leaders must simply posture themselves in strength, but there was nothing left in the tank (at least I didn't think so). On a Sunday night prior to a worship service, I was making my way toward the auditorium. Worship had already begun. I saw a man whom I had never met before standing in the lobby. I stopped to welcome and introduce myself to him. He told me he had a word from the Lord to share with me. I braced myself. I had no idea whether he would bring rebuke or comfort, but I invited him to tell me what he felt the Lord was saying.

He forthrightly quoted from memory the Scripture describing Jesus' answer to the inquiry of John the Baptist's disciples as to whether or not Jesus was the Messiah.

> **Luke 7:22-23 (NKJV)** Jesus answered and said to them, "Go and tell John the things you have seen and heard: that *the* blind see, *the* lame walk, *the* lepers are cleansed, *the* deaf hear, *the* dead are raised, *the* poor have the gospel preached to them. And blessed is *he* who is not offended because of Me."

When he spoke the last phrase "blessed is he who is not offended because of Me" my heart was distinctly struck by God's Holy Spirit. This man went on to say that the Lord's message to me was to not be offended at what He was doing, nor be offended by those who were offended at what God was doing, but to be strong. I had to fight back emotion because this word ministered so strongly and specifically to me at that time. I thanked him, told him that I trusted that he would be ministered to during the worship service and said that I had to get into the service because I was late. My mind certainly was not on the worship singing that night. During and after the service I looked for this individual, but I did not see him and I have not seen him since.

The Scripture and words spoken to me that night ministered to me in a powerful way. They strengthened and encouraged me and gave me a second wind. There is no way this individual could have known what I was going through at the time. I did not know him, and to my knowledge he did not know me. There is no doubt in my mind the word was from the Lord because of how distinctly it ministered to my heart.

PURPOSE NUMBER TWO:

To Demonstrate God's Personal Omniscient Concern

> **1 Corinthians 14:24-25 (NASB)** But if all prophesy, and an unbeliever or an ungifted man enters, he is convicted by all, he is called to account by all; the secrets of his heart are disclosed; and so he will fall on his face and worship God, declaring that God is certainly among you.

A young man named Saul was going to soon be identified and anointed as Israel's new king. The only problem was that he had no idea this was the case, there had never even been a king in Israel before! But all of this was prophetically disclosed to the prophet Samuel. Saul was minding his own business, on an assignment from his father, looking for some of his father's lost herd. He had not had good fortune in this assignment, so it was recommended he invest in the services of a prophet to help him out. He approached Samuel and didn't even get to ask his question. Samuel already knew. Samuel told him his father's donkeys were safe and that through Saul all of Israel's hopes rested on him (a way of saying he would become king of Israel).

> **1 Samuel 9:18-20 (NLT)** Just then Saul approached Samuel at the gateway and asked, "Can you please tell me where the seer's house is?" "I am the seer!" Samuel replied. "Go on up the hill ahead of me to the place of sacrifice, and we'll eat there together. In the morning I will tell you what you want to know and send you on your way. And don't worry about those donkeys that were lost three days ago, for they have been found. And I am here to tell you that you and your family are the focus of all Israel's hopes."

The next day Saul is anointed as Israel's first king and sent on his way. Saul must have been awed by this word from Samuel regarding His destiny. And it is just like God to specifically and personally speak the prophetic word concerning his father's herd. This might have been a confirming and reassuring word that helped Saul accept the larger word concerning his destiny.

After one of our services I approached a tall young man I had never seen before, who had come forward to receive ministry from a prayer team. As I was approaching him, I truly believed that God was showing me that this young man was struggling in his thought life. But I was getting the impression that God did not see him this way, but recognized his heart's intention. His heart was to honor God with his thought life and he hated the struggle he was in. I felt like God wanted him to know He recognized his heart and his struggles. As I introduced myself to this young man I asked for permission to minister to him. I then told him what I had been impressed with as I was walking toward him. He began to weep and said that it was true. He became convinced of God's love for him and we went to war together in prayer over his struggle. That night he experienced breakthrough and deliverance in the restoration of his thought life. Several months later, I unexpectedly ran into him at a ministry function. He came up to me and said that he had gained victory over his struggle and that his life has never been the same since. I believe it is because he became convinced that God knew the deepest concerns of his heart and that He cared!

PURPOSE NUMBER THREE:

To Give Direction and Courage

Acts 13:1-3 (NLT) Among the prophets and teachers of the church at Antioch of Syria were Barnabas, Simeon (called "the black man"), Lucius (from Cyrene), Manaen (the childhood companion of King Herod Antipas), and Saul. One day as these men were worshiping the Lord and fasting, the Holy Spirit said, "Dedicate Barnabas and Saul for the special work I have for them." So after more fasting and prayer, the men laid their hands on them and sent them on their way.

1 Timothy 1:18-19 (NLT) Timothy, my son, here are my instructions for you, based on the prophetic words spoken about you earlier. May they give you the confidence to fight well in the Lord's battles. Cling tightly to your faith in Christ, and always keep your conscience clear. For some people have deliberately violated their consciences; as a result, their faith has been shipwrecked.

The early church strategically sent out Paul and Barnabas on a missionary journey as a result of particular direction from the Lord. Wouldn't you like to receive clear and specific direction from the Lord on what to do? Earlier in this book we identified that this is how David conducted his military battles and even determined what town he should move to. How many times do we as believers, or as corporate ministries, go about our business in an unauthorized manner; our hearts are in the right place, but we have never inquired of the Lord? God has strategic designs and plans for us, for His Church; and He desperately desires that we receive direction from Him.

Now that God has opened our eyes as a leadership team to this reality, we take virtually everything to the Lord in prayer to receive His direction. Instead of generating vision or a ministry assignment and asking the Lord to bless it, we first go to the Lord to receive His vision and His ministry assignment. We then pray and act accordingly. It literally is a night and day difference. It is amazing to experience God's power and authority unleashed in entirely new measures due to seeking His face.

Whenever we go on ministry assignments for the Lord, they will be opposed by Satan and his kingdom. We need to be strengthened by words of encouragement during those times. In the First Timothy text, Paul was exhorting and encouraging Timothy by reminding him of the prophetic words he had earlier received.

We have been on some ministry trips that have been so opposed that we wondered whether or not we ever should have gone. Then, we remembered the tested word we had received concerning the trip, and stayed the course. Later we experienced significant ministry breakthroughs. In those dark times of doubt, those words have been an anchor. Without them, we would have been tempted to give up.

PURPOSE NUMBER FOUR:

To Prepare for Difficulties and Trials

> **Acts 20:22-23 (NLT)** "And now I am going to Jerusalem, drawn there irresistibly by the Holy Spirit, not knowing what awaits me, except that the Holy Spirit has told me in city after city that jail and suffering lie ahead.

We see many times throughout Scripture that God warns His people of trials ahead of time. It certainly helps to be forewarned, for then a person or team can be better prepared and equipped to live in a faith-filled manner. Paul knew that an arrest and imprisonment awaited him in Jerusalem and eventually Rome. He was prepared and was unflinching in his faith.

As I mentioned previously, our church body went through a very difficult several years as God was doing His work in our midst. Before any of the difficulties really broke out, we received one of our first prophetic words. It was a forewarning. On February 18, 2000 we received "A great battle is coming - victory is yours. God is raising up a mighty army. God's Spirit will be poured out on you." Then on March 9, 2000 we received, "Don't fear - only believe; . . . Stay faithful to the Word. Winds of adversity are to blow in from unbelieving Christians - stand strong."

We certainly had no idea what these words meant at the time. Things had been going very well for almost eight years with uninterrupted growth in diverse ways. In fact, I remember when we received these words; I was neither duly impressed nor concerned by them. I had no way of measuring exactly what these words meant. But I cannot tell you how often I referred back to these very same words during the subsequent years of trial. They were a great aid for perspective and strength.

PURPOSE NUMBER FIVE:

To Purify and Sanctify

Acts 5:3-5; 11 (NLT) Then Peter said, "Ananias, why has Satan filled your heart? You lied to the Holy Spirit, and you kept some of the money for yourself. The property was yours to sell or not sell, as you wished. And after selling it, the money was yours to give away. How could you do a thing like this? You weren't lying to us but to God." As soon as Ananias heard these words, he fell to the floor and died. Everyone who heard about it was terrified. . . . Great fear gripped the entire church and all others who heard what had happened.

There were many exciting and amazing occurrences happening in the days of the New Testament Church. Thousands were coming to Christ. There were supernatural healings, along with signs and wonders taking place. A phenomenal characteristic of the early Church was their generous spirit. The people gave away what they possessed to help those in need. It was a natural out-flowing of their love for Christ and one another.

Ananias and Sapphira were a married couple who sold land in order to give the proceeds to the elders to help those in need. They told people they gave it all, but in reality they gave a portion. No one knew but God, and He did not want lying and deceit to be in the DNA of the early Church. God spoke to Peter about it and Peter then paid a visit to Ananias and Sapphira. God exposed Ananias and Sapphira through a prophetic word given to Peter. This couple instantaneously dropped dead due to God's judgment. (How would you like to receive that pastoral visit?)

What is interesting is the line you read in the last part of verse five and verse eleven. *Everyone who heard about it was terrified . . . Great fear gripped the entire church and all others who heard what had happened.* Many followers of Jesus Christ and local churches have developed a fear of man versus a fear of God. We have become market-driven to make sure we attract the crowds versus God-driven to attract the presence and power of God. The beauty of God's holiness needs to be recovered in the Church. God's power and emphasized presence always follow renewed holiness.

After a worship service one Sunday morning, a couple who had attended our church for only a few weeks came up for ministry. Neither my wife nor I knew them, so they introduced themselves. According to their story, the man's ex-wife was harassing them in a relentless and unbearable manner. The picture they painted of his former wife's actions certainly was grounds for sympathy. My wife and I began to pray for them, and my wife received that the man and woman standing before us had been fully involved in a relationship while this man was still married to his former wife. This relationship actually brought an end to his previous marriage. The former wife was hurt and embittered. We asked if what we received was true. They had the candor to admit that this was the case. We then told them that what was done can not be undone (divorce and remarriage to other people), but that they needed to make restitution and make it a priority to care for the legitimate needs of the former wife. They were stunned! They literally had no words to speak as God got right to the source of the issue very quickly. God had revealed to strangers their background and the reason for their difficulties. I do not know if they ever followed through on the directions given to them, because they discontinued attending our church, and I have not seen them since.

It is interesting to read further in Acts chapter five after the story of Ananias and Sapphira. The church advanced and grew! Healthy organisms always do!

> **Acts 5:13-16 (NLT)** No one else dared to join them, though everyone had high regard for them. And more and more people believed and were brought to the Lord—crowds of both men and women. As a result of the apostles' work, sick people were brought out into the streets on beds and mats so that Peter's shadow might fall across some of them as he went by. Crowds came in from the villages around Jerusalem, bringing their sick and those possessed by evil spirits, and they were all healed.

It is not uncommon for the Lord to reveal sin in someone's life that needs to be discontinued and replaced with righteous living. People in our church do live with a healthy fear of knowing that God very likely could and would reveal disobedience in their lives. But the spirit in our church is not oppressed and suppressed; instead it is filled with vibrant life and joy. Repentance is all about God's love for us and our people are more and more living in this reality.

If all this talk of "revealing sin" is making you nervous, don't be. Let me give you a practical side note. It is important to know we do not impose "Ananias and Sapphira words" on people, but instead we say, "This is what we received - is it true?" There is no "thus saith the Lord" words. Also, we never correct someone in a church discipline manner based solely on a prophetic word, but instead on objective evidence. Prophetic disclosure is a gift from God, one that must be monitored by spiritual leaders within the church who can give wisdom and oversight in its application.

PURPOSE NUMBER SIX:

Evangelistic Ministry

> **John 4:17-19; 39 (NLT)** "I don't have a husband," the woman replied. Jesus said, "You're right! You don't have a husband—for you have had five husbands, and you aren't even married to the man you're living with now." "Sir," the woman said, "you must be a prophet." Many Samaritans from the village believed in Jesus because the woman had said, "He told me everything I ever did!"

> **1 Corinthians 14:24-25 (NASB)** But if all prophesy, and an unbeliever or an ungifted man enters, he is convicted by all, he is called to account by all; the secrets of his heart are disclosed; and so he will fall on his face and worship God, declaring that God is certainly among you.

In the account of the Samaritan woman we read how Jesus penetrated her heart by prophetically revealing her life-story. She, an unbeliever, then was convinced of Jesus' message that He was the Messiah. She was so convinced of it that she began to tell others. As a church we are beginning to use the prophetic in evangelistic ministry to unbelievers.

A friend of mine had a breakfast meeting with an international businessperson. This person was not a believer, he confessed to being a pluralistic agnostic (all religions are good because every person and culture needs a religion; yet God could not be personally known). My friend and others had dialogued with him about Jesus and His gospel claims many times. He was well educated and widely experienced. He was very wealthy and influential. My friend asked if I would attend a meeting with this man with the intention of sharing the gospel. This man was a stranger to me; all I knew was that he was an international businessman.

Before I left for the meeting, my wife and I asked the Lord to speak to us about this man. I wanted to be prepared for the meeting; equipped with a message that the Lord was alive and He knew this man intimately. We received that the man currently was living with an extremely burdened heart. The Lord spoke to three major causes of heartache. First, the demands of his business and family were in conflict and he felt overwhelmed and fatigued with reconciling all the demands. Second, he was distressed over the fact that his wife was recently diagnosed with a possibly life-threatening illness. Third, his mother (to whom he was extremely close) was very sick with a life-threatening disease. Then the Lord, in His grace, gave us one more word for good measure; this revelation would immediately reveal the Lord knew Him intimately. We received that this man had recently purchased a luxury sailing boat.

We ended up meeting for breakfast, and we introduced ourselves during conversation, though he stayed guarded and didn't reveal much about himself. He was respectful but did not demonstrate any significant, friendly interest toward me. As conversation went on, I had an opportunity to tell him my wife and I had a chance to pray for him, and that we would continue to do so. I told him about what we had received in prayer regarding his problem with the fatigue and pressure of balancing business and family responsibilities. He did not respond at all, in fact, he seemed rather indifferent to what I had said.

Several minutes later I told him about my family,

and asked him if he had any family. He went to tell me about his four children and wife. I told him that when Cindy and I prayed, we received that his wife had recently been diagnosed with a disease that was causing him great concern. I told him that we of course had no way of knowing for certain whether this was true, but that this is what we received in prayer. Again, he made no response to what I said.

I went on to ask him if his parents were alive. He responded yes, that they were in vibrant health and he enjoyed getting to see them.. Needless to say, at this point I didn't know if we were anywhere on the same planet regarding anything I had shared, let alone in the same zip code. He stated that his parents were in "vibrant health." I quickly debated in my mind whether I should go on. Should I tell him what we had received in prayer about his mother? I figured I was in so deep anyway - let's go for broke! I told him (you guessed it), that we had received that his mother was not in good health, and that he was burdened for her well-being (yes after he had just made a comment to the contrary). He quickly turned toward me and said, "This is too much information! How do you know this?" I knew at that point the Lord had penetrated the deepest recesses of his heart. I told him that we prayed that God would speak to us so that he would know that the Lord loves him and knows him intimately. I told him we only know this information because God told us.

But I knew the Lord had given one more arrow to shoot, so I set it in the bow and drew it back. I asked him what he did for recreation; how he relaxed to help cope with all the pressure. He said that he took up golf a couple of years ago. Being a mediocre golfer myself, I joked with him that golf, more times than not, adds stress instead of releasing it! By his response I knew he was a golfer. I then asked him if he enjoyed any water sports or activity (you can probably guess what I was getting at). He was quick to point out that you had to travel a long distance to get to water from his home and the city where his business was headquartered (which was true). I proceeded to jump in with both feet. Why hold back now? I told him that we had received that he recently had purchased a nice sailing boat. He asked, "How do you know that - did you also receive that in prayer?" I pulled out a small piece of paper from the inside pocket of my blazer and let him read the notes I had taken from our prayer time. It was all there in black and white. He looked at me and finally released a small smile. He admitted to recently having bought a nice sailing vessel.

I told him that the Lord Jesus Christ is alive. I told him that Jesus knew all of the intimate details of his life. He quickly interrupted me, and began talking for fifteen to twenty minutes on the different religions of the worlds and the great religious leaders and philosophers of the world. He was well educated and he articulated his historical knowledge very well. I listened to him and when there was a breathe in the conversation I said, "All the other religions and religious leaders don't even know or even care that you exist for they are dead and can do nothing for you. But Jesus Christ, God the Son, is alive and knows the deepest recesses of your heart and even more importantly cares for you and loves you." I then spent the next five minutes explaining to him the gospel of Jesus Christ. I could tell he was deep in thought.

When I finished explaining the gospel, I asked him if he would like to receive Jesus Christ as his Lord and Savior. He was quiet for what seemed like five minutes but I am sure was not longer than sixty seconds. He then looked up at me and said that he wasn't ready for that commitment (he did understand it was a commitment). But he went on to say that he had just experienced the most powerful argument for the claims of Jesus he had every encountered. The prophetic is a powerful tool in sharing the good news of God's love for mankind.

A WARNING - THE PROPHETIC IS NOT BE USED TO ESTABLISH DOCTRINE

There are many strategic purposes for the prophetic, but I must issue one warning. **The prophetic is not to be used for establishing doctrine.** God has given us the Scriptures for our doctrine. And our doctrine is derived from the Scriptures by good old-fashioned study and by faithfully and proficiently using tools for a competent exegesis (interpretation). Do not even begin to entertain someone's teaching if it is not solidly based and rooted in the sure Word of God!

CHAPTER 9

METHODS OF REVELATION

I have asked my wife, Cindy, to write this next section. The Lord has gifted her in the prophetic and consequently she is able to speak with greater authority on the different ways in which God speaks.

I grew up in a strong Christian home and church where the scriptures were taught and highly valued. The scriptures were more than just something for the mind, they were practically applied in daily life and obedience. I believed from a young age that all the stories and accounts in the Bible were real and factual. I certainly believed that the God of the Scriptures was alive and still concerned about mankind and each one of us as individuals. I was taught the value of prayer as well as repentance. I grew up with a love and an interest in the biblical characters and their lives, and how the Lord used so many of them in powerful ways for His purposes.

I was also taught that miracles and the supernatural work of God was not a part of God's economy for the Christian today. It was as a young adult that I began to dig into the Scriptures and challenge that belief system. If God said He was the same yesterday, today and forever, then surely that must mean He was capable of the same things today. Was I ever delighted when I found out that the very same God of the Old Testament is also the God of the Now; though my life-experience did not reflect this truth to a great extent.

The Lord has allowed me to hear His voice distinctly in diverse ways. It has been through impressions, dreams, visions, trances, His Word, an angelic visitation, verbal words of the Lord and certainly other believers. I would never want to return to the "old days and old ways," it's just too fun and exciting to think that the very Creator of this Universe wants to and loves to converse with me!

His Good Spirit has taught me many things that I would have never thought possible, and on occasion has allowed me to participate in some powerful things for His kingdom. Some of the lessons I learned over these past several years have been difficult and challenging. The Lord always has a plan in mind, and has used these experiences to shape me for His purposes. I certainly do not see myself as an expert on any subject, but just a normal person who wants God to use her in a super-natural and powerful way for His kingdom and His glory. The following are some ways I have experienced God speak to me. I hope this is an encouragement to you as you seek to hear God's voice in greater measure.

METHODS OF REVELATION

IMPRESSION

simple, but can be very powerful.

Biblical Account: Paul
Acts 20:22 (NIV) "And now, compelled by the Spirit, I am going to Jerusalem, not knowing what will happen to me there."

This is a gentle feeling you have in your inner person. It is not precise and sometimes it is hard to articulate exactly what it is that you are sensing. However, there is no doubt that it is the Spirit of the Lord. And you do understand what the Lord is saying to you in a general, broad-brushed manner.

VISIONS

seeing with the eyes of your heart, a snapshot or still image; and/or several frames that are continuous and linked, like watching a movie.

Biblical Account: <u>Stephen</u>

Acts 7:56 (NIV) "Look," he said, "I see heaven open and the Son of Man standing at the right hand of God."

Biblical Account: <u>Daniel</u>

Daniel 7:2 (NIV) Daniel said: "In my vision at night I looked, and there before me were the four winds of heaven churning up the great sea. Four great beasts, each different from the others, came up out of the sea."

These are seen in your "mind's eye." A picture or even a small "video" will be shown. You will be just a "viewer" (Like going to the movies, you watch but not participate). These images many times are similar to having a memory come to your mind. Or it might be comparable to waking up after a dream and you are seeing the images of the dream as you recount it to someone. Or, you also might "see the scenes" vividly in your mind as if you are watching a high definition television.

<u>TRANCE</u>

vision in which you are playing an active role and interfacing in the vision.

Biblical Account: Peter

Acts 10:9-10 (NIV) About noon the following day as they were on their journey and approaching the city, Peter went up on the roof to pray. He became hungry and wanted something to eat, and while the meal was being prepared, he fell into a trance.

If you read this account in its context you see that Peter was actually interacting with the Lord in this trance. I believe that this can distinguish a trance from a vision.

One time when we were asked to pray for a man who was dying with lung cancer, we went to the Lord in prayer to ask whether or not it was the Lord's purpose for Mike and I to pray for him. As we were praying, a story in the Gospels where Jesus healed the man with the crippled hand came to my mind. At this point the account became like a movie, except I was standing next to Jesus watching as it happened. As the Lord reached out His hand to heal the man, He took my hand with His and we touched the man together and he was healed. The Lord made it clear to us that we were to pray for this man's healing. When we arrived to pray for the man, whom we had never met before, I was shocked to see that this was the very man I saw in the trance. Not only did the Lord give us the green light to pray for the man with cancer, the Lord also healed him of that cancer!

DREAMS

similar characteristics as the ways mentioned above, only while sleeping.

Biblical Account: Joseph

> **Matthew 1:20 (NIV)** But after he had considered this, an angel of the Lord appeared to him in a dream and said, "Joseph son of David, do not be afraid to take Mary home as your wife, because what is conceived in her is from the Holy Spirit."

The Scriptures are full of accounts of how God communicated with people through dreams. We many times recount the great story when God asked King Solomon for what he desired. His response was that he might have great wisdom. God made a covenant with Solomon promising that he would be a man of great wisdom, and also a man of great wealth. Seldom do we remember that this covenant transaction took place between him and the Lord in *a dream*! Yet, we see this covenant totally fulfilled in Solomon's life.

Joseph, the earthly father of Jesus, was given directions concerning how he was to handle Mary's pregnancy though she was a virgin. It was also through dreams that he received instruction for providing safety to his wife Mary and the child Jesus. In fact, every time Joseph is mentioned in the Scriptures it is in the context of a dream. I would encourage you to look at the dreams people in the Bible had and their fulfillment, it is amazing!

Do you realize that the Scriptures say that God gives us dreams at night because sometimes when He speaks to us we don't hear Him because our days are frantic? That is what it says in Job.

> **Job 33:14-17 (NLT)** But God speaks again and again, though people do not recognize it. He speaks in dreams, in visions of the night when deep sleep falls on people as they lie in bed. He whispers in their ear and terrifies them with His warning. He causes them to change their minds; he keeps them from pride.

I have found that often I am so "busy" with daily life that sometimes I lose the edge to hear the Lord during my day. Then, I will go to bed and pray a little prayer asking the Lord to speak to me through my dreams if there was something He wanted to say during the day that I didn't hear. Do you know what's amazing? Many times He will! I then have the responsibility to go back and ask the Lord to uncover the mystery He gave me in the dream. I ask if there are any action steps I need to obey, or insight He wants me to have. Since He is the giver of those dreams, I can be assured He will answer me. I don't believe the Lord is playing games with us; He truly wants us to know.

ANGELIC REVELATION

God communicates through an angel, whether asleep or awake.

Biblical Account: Lot

> **Genesis 19:1(NIV)** The two angels arrived at Sodom in the evening, and Lot was sitting in the gateway of the city. When he saw them, he got up to meet them and bowed down with his face to the ground.

As I stated earlier, I believe every account in scripture. But there is a huge difference between reading about an encounter, and actually having one yourself.

On February 16, 2000 I went to bed just like you probably do, fairly exhausted and hoping for a good night's sleep. However, on this night, little did I know my life would be changed forever.

I live in a small town in Washington State; nothing spectacular, just like thousands of little towns scattered across the United States. I am the mother of two daughters and had been married for 24 years at the time. I live in a very normal middle class house in a middle class neighborhood. All my friends, personal family, and church family have no claim to fame. We would be what you would call "average" people. The reason I emphasize this is because of the following account. It could happen to anyone, anytime, and anyplace, according to God's will.

I woke up to a very bright light shining in my eyes. The kind you can see even though your eyes are closed. I first thought that my youngest daughter had come home late from her job (she worked the swing shift) and accidentally left the hall light on. This often was the case.

I laid there a few minutes with my eyes closed deciding whether or not to get up and turn off the light. Finally, I could stand it no longer, and sat up leaning on my elbows a little disgusted that my good sleep had been interrupted. As I opened my eyes to get out of bed, something inside me knew this wasn't the hall light. This light had a bright, luminous glow to it and I knew it was different than anything of which I was familiar.

It was then that I noticed two very large beings at the foot of the bed about six feet away. They both had dark hair and eyes. They also were very muscular (way more than any human I have ever seen) and were as high as the ceiling, which was eight feet. Their heads were up by the ceiling, but their legs disappeared at their thighs into the floor (our house was two stories). These beings, which I now know were angels, where dressed in a fashion like a Roman soldier would be. They had a very serious look on their faces like they had been sent on "business."

At this point I thought I was dreaming. These things don't happen to every day common people, least of all me. I was full of conflicting emotions, trying to figure out what I was experiencing, and praying that I wasn't being deceived by evil spirits. My human mind was not able to grasp what my eyes were seeing, but my spirit was telling me it was true. I was so terrified that I had to tell myself to breathe. I cannot adequately describe how overwhelmed I felt.

As I stared, not believing what I was seeing, I

noticed they were holding something that reflected the light. As I looked I noticed huge swords in their hands. They looked like they were standing at attention with the swords across their chests. The swords were double-edged and appeared to be six to seven feet long - they were huge.

By this time, I thought I had better wake my husband up, but I found myself frozen against any and all movement. I also noticed a light coming from a source on my side of the bed that was reflected off one of the swords of the two angels. At this point my spirit had convinced my mind that this indeed was real! Funny, I found myself thinking that if I looked over next to me, I might see the Lord, and die right where I sat!

I felt compelled to look, almost like I had to, and there I found another angel. He was dressed in a glistening white robe, trimmed in a beautiful gold band around the sleeves and neck. The gold appeared to be glistening as well. This angel had light colored hair and the most amazing and beautiful eyes. I have never seen eyes like those, they were blue and green and clear. They were like a clear mountain river shining in the summer sun. But it was the love that emanated from those eyes, it was deep and pure, like one could fall into that love and be swept away. It was like I was being drawn into those eyes.

By now I could take no more, so I laid back down and closed my eyes only to wake up and find it morning. I got up and made my way into the bathroom in our bedroom to shower and get ready for work, all the while, contemplating and praying about what had happened in the night. (My husband, Mike, was already up and downstairs having his time with the Lord.)

I had gotten dressed and was drying my hair, when I felt the Lord compel me to stop and step out into the bedroom, which I promptly did. As I did, I noticed the angel in white, who I had seen the night before, standing at the foot of my bed. I immediately fell to my knees and then to my stomach on the floor.

I was weeping heavily, because I could feel the holiness, yet at the same time my own humanity and sinfulness was so obvious to me. I stayed in that position for about twenty minutes. Finally, the angel spoke, and a great fear seized me. I felt I would die because of the holiness I felt around me. He spoke so gently and kindly, and told me to get up off of the floor. With great trembling I got to my knees, for I could go no further. He then told me he had been sent by the Lord with a message, a message that soon would be revealed. He also said in the coming days that the Lord would teach me and train my ear to hear His voice in ways I never had before.

The angel then left and I felt a peace, yet a seriousness to what had and was going to transpire. I knew that I had been given something very special to steward and use for the Lord.

I now understand that at salvation I was given the gift of the prophetic, I also believe this is when the Lord fully released it in my life.

In the days that followed, the Lord indeed began to speak. At first I assumed the thoughts that were entering my head must be myself, but then I realized I could never know on my own the things that were revealed. Also, during prayer sessions with other people I did not know, the Lord would reveal things to me that only that person and God would know. When I would share what I received from the Lord with the people, they would agree that the disclosure was true and also would be totally amazed - along with me!

The Lord began to speak to me about some amazing things that He was going to be doing. Mike and I both wrestled with "Can all of this be true?" Then one day I received a word about a healing the Lord was going to do in a public way, and that this healing would authenticate that indeed what I was hearing was from the Lord. The Lord spoke as to who the person was that He was going to heal. It would be miraculous and it was a staff person and elder of our church, who had a young family. He had been very ill with an irreversible, terminal disease. That healing did take place - in the most amazing way!

So, does the Lord still send angels today to average people? I would have to say a resounding "Yes!" This is to be addressed with great care and discernment when it does happen, for we are familiar with the many deceptions that have come to mankind through false spirits, spirits who presented themselves as angels of light. But at the same time, the Scriptures are filled with angelic appearances to men and women, and God still works through His angelic beings to accomplish much of His work with mankind.

AUDIBLE VOICE

Biblical Account: Paul

> **Acts 9:4 (NIV)** He fell to the ground and heard a voice say to him, "Saul, Saul, why do you persecute me?"

There are many accounts in Scripture where God spoke to mankind with words that could be heard with the natural ear. Certainly Paul was one of those men.

In the middle of the night, on October 23, 2000, I was awakened by a voice that said, "George Bush and Gary Locke are my men for the hour" (Gary Locke was running for governor of the state of Washington). Thinking that my husband Mike was talking in his sleep, I ignored it and tried to go back to sleep. Then, about ten minutes later, I heard the same exact statement again. That really got my attention! Now in the middle of the night I'm not the sharpest tack in the box, but something in my spirit told me what I heard was real, and not just my mind, and it wasn't Mike. So, as I lay there I began to ponder what was said. On November 2nd, we Americans would be voting in a new president, and the citizens of Washington State would vote in a new governor for our state. I figured that the Lord must know something I didn't!

The next morning, I told Mike what I heard in the middle of the night, and he said "Humph, that's interesting." (At this point, I'm sure Mike thought his wife had slipped over that fine line!) If you remember anything about November of 2000, you will recall all the hoopla that surrounded the election of George W. Bush. The ballots in Florida were counted a couple gazillion times with perpetual confusion as to who won the election.

Each time the situation would come up on the news, I would get frustrated and say to Mike, "Well, I don't care what it looks like or who says what, the Lord said Bush was the man for the hour." At which Mike would then reply jokingly, "Not everyone has been told that!" And you know the rest of the story, Bush did become President and for those who are not familiar with Washington State politics, Gary Locke won the election for Washington!

SCRIPTURES

Biblical Account: Daniel

Daniel 9:2-3 (NIV) in the first year of his reign, I, Daniel, understood from the Scriptures, according to the word of the LORD given to Jeremiah the prophet, that the desolation of Jerusalem would last seventy years. So I turned to the Lord God and pleaded with Him in prayer and petition, in fasting, and in sackcloth and ashes.

All of us have experienced hearing God's voice in this way. It's those times when you are reading along and suddenly the verse just "jumps off the page." Then you begin to ponder and meditate on what the Lord is communicating to you. Or you're out driving along and, for "no reason whatsoever," a verse or portion of scripture pops into your mind. Don't ignore it; the Lord is speaking to your heart. Listen closely, He has something to say.

GOD USES OTHER PEOPLE

Biblical Account: Simeon

Luke 2:25; 33-35 (NLT) Now there was a man named Simeon who lived in Jerusalem. He was a righteous man and very devout. He was filled with the Holy Spirit, and he eagerly expected the Messiah to come and rescue Israel. Joseph and Mary were amazed at what was being said about Jesus. Then Simeon blessed them, and he said to Mary, "This child will be rejected by many in Israel, and it will be their undoing. But he will be the greatest joy to many others. Thus, the deepest thoughts of many hearts will be revealed. And a sword will pierce your very soul."

Biblical Account: Ananias

Acts 9:10; 11; 15 (NLT) Now there was a believer in Damascus named Ananias. The Lord spoke to him in a vision, calling, "Ananias!" "Yes, Lord!" he replied. The Lord said, "Go over to Straight Street, to the house of Judas. When you arrive, ask for Saul of Tarsus. He is praying to Me right now. . . " But the Lord said, "Go and do what I say. For Saul is my chosen instrument to take my message to the Gentiles and to kings, as well as to the people of Israel."

Many times the Lord relays messages through other people. The Scriptures are filled with such instances. Sometimes the people He uses are not even aware of speaking prophetically. Those who do know, often have been given a word of encouragement or even some scripture to share with us (refer back to Mike's story of the man in the foyer who spoke to Mike before an evening service).

Remember, we are to test the words we receive

from others, so we will not be confused or deceived. Mike covers those guidelines later in this book. Also, when we believe we have received something from the Lord for another person, our only responsibility is to deliver those words in love (1 Corinthians 13). We are not responsible to see if the person receives or even acts on what we give them. That is solely up to them before the Lord.

SUMMARY

These are just some of the ways we can experience the Lord speaking to us, and by no means is it meant to be an exhaustive list. We do need to cultivate listening to the Lord; like learning to ride a bike, each time we do it, it becomes easier.

As you grow in hearing the Lord's voice it will grow your faith by leaps and bounds. It will encourage you in your walk with the Lord, and will strengthen your heart and your understanding of just how much our heavenly Father loves to converse with us. I love what our brother David wrote in Psalm 27:8. "My heart has heard you say, 'Come and talk with Me' and my heart responds, 'Lord, I am coming.'"

Mike is going to jump in and present some truths and principles that will help protect us from deception and error.

CHAPTER 10

PROTECTION FROM DECEPTION AND ERROR

Safeguarding the prophetic from deception and error is another component of this subject that is very broad and this book is not designed to comprehensively cover it. As I previously mentioned, the prophetic has been discredited many times because it was poorly handled and not given strong and proper leadership. Consequently, God and His ways have at times been misrepresented. We must honestly confess that there have been messes throughout church history surrounding the prophetic. But that is no reason to discredit, ignore, or despise the prophetic. I have a friend who pointed out an insightful verse to me found in the book of Proverbs.

> **Proverbs 14:4 (NASB)** Where no oxen are, the manger is clean, But much revenue *comes* by the strength of the ox.

This verse basically is saying that if you want a clean stable, don't buy an ox. But it is through the ox that you make your livelihood. Therefore, you have a decision to make. You can have a clean stable and go hungry, or you can have income with an ox that dirties the stable. Now, you have to clean the stable! Things can get messy with the prophetic, but that doesn't mean we throw it out.

The prophetic is an absolutely strategic and powerful weapon for the kingdom of God, but every once in a while you might have to clean up a mess. But, isn't that true with every ministry within a church? How about the worship ministry in a church - have you ever had a mess there? How about youth ministry or children's ministry? We don't give up on worship when there is a problem, nor the children's ministry. Those who work in business - have you ever had a mess between the sales force and accounting? You can't just give up on one division or another because of problems. Your business would go under. So it is with the prophetic ministry in the Church of Jesus Christ. We can't afford a clean stall. We need the ox of the prophetic to work in the fields of our lives and ministries. But there are principles and truths that we can employ to minimize potential messes. How can we minimize deception and error? There are some fundamental truths and principles we will cover.

STEP 1 – PREPARATION OF THE PERSON

There are three sources from which prophetic messages originate or are influenced. The first is

God. Second is the demonic kingdom. And third is our natural man, also known as our sinful nature. We want to minimize and eliminate the demonic and our sinful nature from bringing mixture into hearing God's voice.

We must begin by safeguarding our lives, for God speaks to and through human beings. We must close every door of access that we might give to Satan and his minions. In our booklet "Stongholds" and "One World Two Realms," we address the issue of Satan gaining access and influence in our lives by providing him with a *topos* (rightful place of jurisdiction) or *strongholds* (base of operations). A *topos* or *stronghold* basically is afforded to Satan when there is anything in our lives that does not line up with God's truth. To safeguard our lives we must begin by setting ourselves apart from sin and any alliances with Satan. We then must align ourselves with God's truth.

The following are some examples of how we can provide access or form alliances with Satan by our life-style. The more ground we give to our enemy, the more vulnerable we are to demonic influence, which hinders God's voice. Likewise, this also will give our sinful nature a platform to influence us in hearing God's voice. Not only are these doors of access, but they are filters through which we receive and communicate. For example, if the Lord gives me a message for someone, but I have a stronghold of anger in my life, the way in which I communicate the message will be through the lens of anger. The message might be right but it is received and communicated in a wrong spirit, which in essence misrepresents the message. I am sure you have had someone present a truth to you with the wrong spirit; you knew what they were saying was the truth, but it had an edge of anger, bitterness, or fear.

The following are sins (or strongholds) that the Scriptures distinctly link with Satan and the demonic kingdom.

Anger, Unforgiveness, Resentment

Ephesians 4.26-27 (NASB) BE ANGRY, AND yet DO NOT SIN; do not let the sun go down on your anger, and do not give the devil an opportunity.

2 Corinthians 2:10-11 (NASB) But whom you forgive anything, I forgive also; for indeed what I have forgiven, if I have forgiven anything, I did it for your sakes in the presence of Christ, in order that no advantage be taken of us by Satan; for we are not ignorant of his schemes.

Do you live with any unforgiveness, any resentment, and/or anger? Is there any person, situation, or institution that you hold a grudge against due to being violated or betrayed?

Sexual Immorality/perversion

> **1 Corinthians 5:1, 5 (NASB)** It is actually reported that there is immorality among you, and immorality of such a kind as does not exist even among the Gentiles, that someone has his father's wife. . . . I have decided to deliver such a one to Satan for the destruction of his flesh, that his spirit may be saved in the day of the Lord Jesus.

Let's examine our lives on this one. We live in a society in which we can easily become calloused and insensitive to sexual immorality. This immorality includes everything that is in contrast to God's design for sexuality. Men, how is your thought life? Where do your eyes wander? To be unrepentant in this area is to place yourself in the realm of Satan's influence.

Hatred, violence, disunity, lying

> **Luke 9:54-56 (NASB)** And when His disciples James and John saw this, they said, "Lord, do You want us to command fire to come down from heaven and consume them?" But He turned and rebuked them,

and said, "You do not know what kind of spirit you are of; for the Son of Man did not come to destroy men's lives, but to save them."

John 8:44 (NASB) You are of your father the devil, and you want to do the desires of your father. He was a murderer from the beginning, and does not stand in the truth, because there is no truth in him. Whenever he speaks a lie, he speaks from his own nature; for he is a liar, and the father of lies.

These are pretty self-explanatory. Is your life characterized by lying or deceit? How about unity? How do you view others in the body of Christ - including those who belong to the Lord but don't come from your exact theological heritage? Do you wrestle with seeing others as wrong except those in your own little group? Do you struggle with being critical of those with whom you associate?

Jealousy, selfish ambition

James 3:14-16 (NASB) But if you have bitter jealousy and selfish ambition in your heart, do not be arrogant and so lie against the truth. This wisdom is not that which comes down from above, but is earthly, natural, demonic. For where jealousy and selfish ambition exist, there is disorder and every evil thing.

What can be commented on here? Jealousy and selfish ambition is pretty easy to identify. Does everything you do and say have the intent of glorifying God and benefiting others around you? Are you willing to be a nameless and faceless servant of the Lord and others? Do you desire nothing more than to see God glorified and others benefited and prospered by your life and ministry?

Insubordination, rebellious spirit, disobedience to God

> **1 Samuel 15:22-23 (NASB)** And Samuel said, "Has the LORD as much delight in burnt offerings and sacrifices as in obeying the voice of the LORD? Behold, to obey is better than sacrifice, and to heed than the fat of rams. "For rebellion is as the sin of divination, And insubordination is as iniquity and idolatry. Because you have rejected the word of the LORD, He has also rejected you from being king."

The Scriptures say that rebellion enters you into Satan's realm. It is the foundation of Satan's kingdom. Do you live with an independent spirit? Do you qualify your obedience to God or in everything do you immediately, joyfully, and completely obey God? King Saul wanted to obey God on his terms. That is not obedience. Eighty percent obedience is not obedience.

King Saul disobeyed and disregarded what Samuel said. Do you have an insubordinate heart toward others?

Occult Practices

> **Luke 19:31(NASB)** Do not turn to mediums or spiritists; do not seek them out to be defiled by them. I am the LORD your God.

> **Deuteronomy 18:9-13 (NASB)** "When you enter the land which the LORD your God gives you, you shall not learn to imitate the detestable things of those nations. "There shall not be found among you anyone who makes his son or his daughter pass through the fire, one who uses divination, one who practices witchcraft, or one who interprets omens, or a sorcerer, or one who casts a spell, or a medium, or a spiritist, or one who calls up the dead. "For whoever does these things is detestable to the LORD; and because of these detestable things the LORD your God will drive them out before you. "You shall be blameless before the LORD your God.

The Western culture is becoming increasingly inundated with occult influence. Whether it is in the form of movies, books, music, or games; we are being assaulted. Do a thorough examination of your life and home. Is there anything that gives Satan's kingdom the slightest recognition or honor? Destroy it!

Idolatry or Greed

> **1 Corinthians 10:19-20 (NASB)** What do I mean then? That a thing sacrificed to idols is anything, or that an idol is anything? No, but I say that the things which the Gentiles sacrifice, they sacrifice to demons, and not to God; and I do not want you to become sharers in demons.
>
> **Colossians 3:5 (NASB)** Therefore consider the members of your earthly body as dead to immorality, impurity, passion, evil desire, and greed, which amounts to idolatry.

Greed can be so obvious, and at times it is found in the most subtle of coveting forms. Are you generous with what God has given you? Do you freely and regularly tithe your income to God? Do you freely give to others in need (or maybe they are not in desperate need but it would bless them)?

What about idolatry? What is idolatry? Let me offer the following definition for you to measure whether or not there is idolatry in your life. *"Idolatry is having greater affection, or finding greater security in anything or anyone besides God alone."* Do you have any idolatry in your life?

Living In a Violated Conscience

1 Timothy 1:20 (NASB) Among these are Hymenaeus and Alexander, whom I have delivered over to Satan, so that they may be taught not to blaspheme. (Note context of 1:18-20)

Something might or might not be intrinsically right or wrong, but no matter which, for you it is wrong. To participate in it violates your conscience. It can be an area of Christian freedom, but you cannot afford to violate your conscience. It is critical that we protect our consciences and keep them sensitive to the Lord and His Holy Spirit. A violated conscience becomes a beachhead for the demonic and opens us up to greater expressions of sin and we ultimately and consequently become blasphemous toward the Lord.

Worldliness, Gossiping, Sensuality

1 Timothy 5:13-15 (NASB) And at the same time they also learn to be idle, as they go around from house to house; and not merely idle, but also gossips and busybodies, talking about things not proper to mention. Therefore, I want younger widows to get married, bear children, keep house, and give the enemy no occasion for reproach; for some have already turned aside to follow Satan.

Is your life strategically and intentionally lived for God's kingdom and glory? Our lives can at times be marked by idleness and gossiping. When we are involved in vain, useless, and destructive activities, we are open to the enemy's influence and assault in our lives. Being worldly, idle, a gossip, or a busybody cannot be tolerated in God's economy!

Pride

> **Isaiah 14:13-15 (NASB)** "But you said in your heart, 'I will ascend to heaven; I will raise my throne above the stars of God, and I will sit on the mount of assembly in the recesses of the north. 'I will ascend above the heights of the clouds; I will make myself like the Most High.' "Nevertheless you will be thrust down to Sheol, to the recesses of the pit."

Pride is synonymous with selfishness. Everything revolves around us. We are self-absorbed. Pride breeds murmuring and complaining, jealousy and envy, offense and disunity. Note the "I wills. . ." in the previous verses - evidencing Satan's real heart that led to his ruin.

This is why Philippians 2 says that we are to be humble like Christ. This humility is seen in a life that always puts others first. We are not to be concerned with making good impressions. Our job is to constantly be seeking to help and benefit others.

When we read the previous verses closely we see that each of those sins have an association with Satan's kingdom. So we need to keep close surveillance on our lives. The more these sins have access to our lives, the more vulnerable we are to mixture and influence of the demonic and our sinful nature. I know there are more sins that the Scriptures directly identify as having an association with the demonic; but these will get us thinking and moving in the right direction. In fact, right now let's take a little evaluation of our lives and see how we are doing in terms of giving access to the demonic kingdom and our natural flesh.

OPEN DOOR OF SIN & SINFUL NATURE	Holy Spirit Controlled	It's a Struggle	It Controls Me
Anger, Unforgiveness, Resentment			
Sexual immorality/perversion			
Hatred, violence, disunity, lying			
Jealousy, selfish ambition			
Insubordination, rebellious/ independent spirit, disobedience to God			
Occult Practices			
Idolatry or greed			
Living In a Violated Conscience			
Worldliness, gossiping, sensuality			
Pride			

We are not talking about being able to live sinless lives, but about having a pure heart that seeks to love the Lord with everything we've got. Our desire is to love Him with all our heart, soul, mind, and strength. If we truly love the Lord, our constant desire is to obey Him. We want to live in a continual state of repentance so that if anything in our life violates the heart and will of God, we will, without hesitation, get right with Him. Then we will shut the doors of access to the demonic and suppress the influence of our sinful nature. The booklet, *Strongholds,* would be a good place to start in dismantling any demonic access in our life.

STEP 2 – PREPARATION FOR YOUR PRAYER TIME

The Scriptures speak clearly to the authority we are given in Christ authority at salvation. We describe this in our booklet *One World – Two Realms: Operating in Christ's Authority*. In it, we address the Scriptures that speak to the fact that Jesus is seated at the right hand of God the Father, far above all rulers and authorities of the spirit world. At salvation the follower of Jesus Christ enters into that authority by being raised up with Christ, seated with Him at the Father's right hand in the heavenlies realm. The gospels provide accounts where Jesus specifically gave His disciples power and authority to do ministry in His name. The disciples came back astounded that they ministered the gospel, healed people, and even witnessed demons being subject to them in Jesus' name.

As believers, we need to exercise the authority we have in Jesus Christ. We need to "bind" (or forbid) the "strongman" (Satan) based on the binding work Jesus did through His death and resurrection. We must believe that what Jesus said is true, that we have authority over all the power of the enemy.

Therefore, when it is time for us to pray to hear from God, we ask the Lord to show us anything that will hinder us from hearing Him purely and freely. If there is any sinful attitude or action that is a hindrance, we make a statement of confession and genuine repentance. Then, we exercise Christ's authority given to us, and in Jesus' name, we rebuke any demonic spirit that would try to block, deceive, confuse, or in any way compromise what God wants to say. We also pray that all of our natural man or sinful nature, that would compromise our hearing the Lord, would be completely restricted from interfering with our hearing what God wants to say to us.

First, we must believe that the authority that Christ gave us over the demonic is real, and when exercised in humble righteousness with conviction, business has been done. Second, we must believe that God answers our prayer when we ask that He would not allow our own flesh to conflict with His voice. This is a prayer that is according to God's will. Therefore, we can then go to the Lord in prayer, and in faith believe that what we receive is from the Lord.

STEP 3 – UNDERSTAND THE THREE COMPONENTS OF THE PROPHETIC

The truths of this section have been very strategic for us in our ministry. It has helped protect us from messes, and when things begin to look like they could get messy, we can walk through this process to help bring order. I also want to make it clear that identifying these three components in the prophetic are not original with me, although I can't remember where I first read them. I was helped by reading what Jack Deere wrote about these three components in his book *Surprised by the Voice of God.* Since then, I have seen many biblical examples of these three components.

The three components are first "revelation," second "interpretation," and third "application." "Revelation" simply is what is received from the Lord; whether it is a dream, a vision, words, or any other media by which God communicates to mankind. It is simply the message or revelatory disclosure itself. The "interpretation" component is what is meant by what is said. Another way of stating it is, "What does God want to communicate by the revelation or prophetic disclosure He has given to us?" Lastly, the "application" component is; "What are we to do with the revelation and interpretation we have received?" Or, "How are we to apply what we now understand?"

I can relate this to a pastor who prepares a sermon every week. The pastor has the Scriptures, God's revelation to mankind. This pastor then takes a particular text of the Scriptures, applies principles of interpretation to that text to determine the truth God was communicating to the original audience. This is interpretation. He then takes the truths he has pulled from the scripture and applies them to the contemporary audience.

Let's apply this to the prophetic. What we receive

in prayer simply is the "revelation." We must not understand it to be anything other than revelation. We then must separately address the interpretation of what was received and not jump to conclusions. Many times God speaks in figurative language or prophetic symbols and pictures. We then seek to understand what God is meaning to communicate (whether it be dreams, words and prophetic pictures received in prayer, visions, et cetera). This is the "interpretation component." Then, if and when we believe we have come to understand what God is communicating, we need to separately seek out what are we to do with the revelation and interpretation. This is the "application component." Are we to simply pray on it, are we to put it into action, and if so, when and how?

We have learned by experience that very few times is the prophetic disclosure or revelation wrong. When we have messes, it usually is due to the fact that we have confused and/or not kept separate the three components. We might jump the gun and interpret images or language and end up with an improper application. We must make sure that we keep these three components distinct.

This is illustrated for us many times in the

Scriptures but an account in the book of Acts distinctly demonstrates this for us in the life of Paul and a prophet named Agabus.

> **Acts 20:22-24 (NLT)** "And now I am going to Jerusalem, drawn there irresistibly by the Holy Spirit, not knowing what awaits me, except that the Holy Spirit has told me in city after city that jail and suffering lie ahead. But my life is worth nothing unless I use it for doing the work assigned me by the Lord Jesus—the work of telling others the Good News about God's wonderful kindness and love."

> **Acts 21:10-14 (NLT)** During our stay of several days, a man named Agabus, who also had the gift of prophecy, arrived from Judea. When he visited us, he took Paul's belt and bound his own feet and hands with it. Then he said, "The Holy Spirit declares, 'So shall the owner of this belt be bound by the Jewish leaders in Jerusalem and turned over to the Romans.' " When we heard this, we who were traveling with him, as well as the local believers, begged Paul not to go on to Jerusalem. But he said, "Why all this weeping? You are breaking my heart! For I am ready not only to be jailed at Jerusalem but also to die for the sake of the Lord Jesus." When it was clear that we couldn't persuade him, we gave up and said, "The will of the Lord be done."

In this account we see a revelation had been received by a prophet named Agabus. Agabus discloses what he had received by a demonstration of tying up his hands and feet with Paul's sash. He then states he had received a prophetic disclosure that the owner of the belt will be arrested by Jewish leaders and turned over to the Roman officials. This was obviously an ominous word of danger. Was it a true revelation of God? We know that the revelation was correct, for in the following chapters we do read that Paul was arrested and sent to Rome where he was imprisoned and stood trial.

But we notice the friends that were gathered with Paul jumped to the conclusion that Paul was not to go to Jerusalem. Out of their love for him, they feared for his life, and rightfully so. In this situation we see an example where the three components lose their distinct roles. They assumed an application from the revelation instead of praying and seeking what was to be done in light of the revelation that had been received. Paul refused to be swayed by the persuasion of his friends. He knew that the Holy Spirit had prompted and prepared him for what would lie ahead. He did go to Jerusalem, he was arrested, he did end up in Rome, and it was there that he wrote a major portion of his writings that became New Testament Scriptures.

If you can keep the three components of the prophetic distinct when ministering with the prophetic, you will save yourself many messes! Go before the Lord to understand each component and then move accordingly.

STEP 4 – EMPLOY STRATEGIC PROTECTIVE MEASURES

Operating and ministering in the prophetic is not risky or hazardous if we employ strategic biblical principles. It is when we ignore these principles that we end up with unnecessary confusion, error, and harm.

Principle 1: "You always subject the prophetic to the Scriptures." The Scriptures are the more sure word of prophecy. God's Word is the standard by which everything else is measured and submitted.

> **2 Peter 1:16-21 (NASB)** For we did not follow cleverly devised tales when we made known to you the power and coming of our Lord Jesus Christ, but we were eyewitnesses of His majesty. For when He received

> honor and glory from God the Father, such an utterance as this was made to Him by the Majestic Glory, "This is My beloved Son with whom I am well-pleased" - and we ourselves heard this utterance made from heaven when we were with Him on the holy mountain. *So* we have the prophetic word *made* more sure, to which you do well to pay attention as to a lamp shining in a dark place, until the day dawns and the morning star arises in your hearts. But know this first of all, that no prophecy of Scripture is *a matter* of one's own interpretation, for no prophecy was ever made by an act of human will, but men moved by the Holy Spirit spoke from God.

Peter speaks to an amazing experience when he received revelation as to the future glory that Jesus would receive. Put yourself in his sandals, what must that experience have been like? He witnessed the appearance of Moses and Elijah and watched Jesus be transfigured into a partial measure of His future glory. Then, he heard God the Father give testimony to His pleasure with His Son Jesus Christ. As amazing as that experience must have been, he then speaks to another form of revelation - the written word of God. He states that the prophecy given, the Scriptures, that which was received by the prophets of old is now more sure due to Jesus' testimony. He then exhorts his readers that the Scriptures are established by God. They are not a product of human will. Second Timothy chapter three states that the Scriptures are our standard for righteousness, correction, and equipping.

> **2 Timothy 3:16-17 (NASB)** All Scripture is inspired by God and profitable for teaching, for reproof, for correction, for training in righteousness; so that the man of God may be adequate, equipped for every good work.

One reason the prophetic ministry sometimes goes awry and people become disillusioned and damaged is because we violate this number one principle. The first question we must condition ourselves to ask when we believe that we have received a communiqué from the Lord is, "How does it line up with God's Word?" God will not give a message to us in prayer or a dream that is in contrast or conflict with the truths of His Scriptures. If there is ever a conflict between a subjective revelation received in prayer and the objective revelation of Scriptures - it is the prophetic word that is lacking, not the Scriptures.

Principle 2: "Understand and Respect the Relationship between Prophetic Revelation & Spiritual Authority."

There has been much division and conflict surrounding the prophetic due to this principle being violated. Consequently, this is why many have tried to discredit the prophetic.

Spiritual authority is a foundational principle in the economy of God's kingdom. This subject is broad, deep, and critical. It also has been abused and misused to create fear and skepticism. There is much ignorance, disregard, and misunderstanding surrounding this subject that results in confusion and resistance to this topic. As a result, many Christians, families, churches, and businesses unnecessarily suffer. We do not have the adequate space to address this. We are devoting an entire booklet to the subject of "Spiritual Authority" to more comprehensively address its truths.

The Scriptures have many accounts that demonstrate how God regards those who discount or disregard spiritual authority in their lives. In Numbers chapter twelve Moses' older sister and brother criticized their brother as God's extended and delegated authority.

> **Numbers 12:1-2 (NLT)** While they were at Hazeroth, Miriam and Aaron criticized Moses because he had married a Cushite woman. They said, "Has the LORD spoken only through Moses? Hasn't He spoken through us, too?" But the LORD heard them.

Their accusation was that they heard from the Lord as well as Moses. Why do we have to follow Moses' leadership? He even married a foreign woman. God heard their assault against His spiritual authority. Simply put, God chose Moses to lead. He called them together at the entrance of the Tabernacle (this would be similar to when my father would command me to meet him in his bedroom when I had misbehaved - not a pleasant meeting). The result was that God showed His severe displeasure and discipline toward Miriam by afflicting her with leprosy. God made it clear that her actions against Moses were actions toward Him. This was a devastating disease that resulted in disability and social isolation. The Scriptures register that God was furious with Miriam and Aaron.

> **Numbers 12:7; 9; 10 (NLT)** "But that is not how I communicate with My servant Moses. He is entrusted with My entire house." The LORD was furious with them, and He departed. As the cloud moved from above the Tabernacle, Miriam suddenly became white as snow with leprosy. . . .

We read of a similar account in Numbers chapter sixteen with men named Korah, Dathan, and Abiram. They did not seem to learn from God's displeasure with Miriam because of her attitude and actions against Moses. These leaders in Israel assaulted Moses with similar accusations as had Miriam. God's response of displeasure and discipline toward them was even more severe than it was toward Miriam. God warned the rest of Israel to separate themselves from these three men. Then, for the first time in human history, God opened up the earth, swallowed these men and their households, and shut the earth back up again.

God has extended His authority on earth through mankind. The Scriptures speak to the role of husbands, parents, local church leaders, government leaders, and employers. God leads and directs through His extended authority in human leaders. The Lord makes it clear that leaders will give an account for how they exercise God's authority. Leaders are responsible to represent God, His truth, His will, and His ways in their leadership and toward those they lead. And we will give an answer to the Lord for how we submit to and follow those God has placed over us.

> **Hebrews 13:17 (NLT)** Obey your spiritual leaders and do what they say. Their work is to watch over your souls, and they know they are accountable to God. Give them reason to do this joyfully and not with sorrow. That would certainly not be for your benefit.

The Scriptures also make it clear that those who receive prophetic disclosures from the Lord can and are to control themselves. When people receive a revelation from the Lord they are to minister their gift in a submissive spirit.

> **1 Corinthians 14:32-33 (NLT)** Remember that people who prophesy are in control of their spirit and can wait their turn. For God is not a God of disorder but of peace, as in all the other churches.

There is much more that can and needs to be said on this subject, but let me summarize the truths of this principle. If you are unwilling to live your life in interdependent community with other believers in a local church, and if you live with an independent, insubordinate attitude toward spiritual leaders and authority in your life, you make yourself vulnerable to demonic deception. Such an attitude and lifestyle is an expression of arrogance and pride. James 4 states that God opposes the proud, it is the humble person to whom He gives His favor and grace.

To help safeguard from error in hearing God's voice, you must recognize how God regards spiritual authority. You must willingly submit your life and be willing to submit any revelation you receive to your spiritual authority; your pastors, elders, vicars, priests, et cetera. When necessary, you then must release your revelation to be used according to the discretion of your spiritual authority. They will give an answer to the oversight and leadership of the church—not you. There are some who have the gift of the prophetic who believe that they are in a place of preeminence over the pastors or elders in the church. They expect to be able to influence the church and its leaders due to "hearing from the Lord." I know of stories where people received a "word from the Lord" for the church, but the pastor (who believed in the prophetic) did not believe the revelation was of God. The one who received the word immediately left the church when his word was not received and given to the church. This man's insubordinate, self-willed heart was exposed. I applaud the pastor who takes responsibility for the leadership of the church.

Leaders, this ministry must receive strong leadership. The enemy will do everything possible to derail and discredit this amazing blessing and powerful weapon God has given to us. We can't be intimidated when someone comes up and says, "I received from the Lord. . . " We must test and measure everything, and provide strong, biblical, Holy Spirit-filled leadership. God's design is for us to be a major factor in protecting the prophetic from error. Let's fulfill our role with humble confidence and conviction!

Principle 3: "<u>Employ Proven Principles to Interpret the Revelation You Receive</u>." We must remember that it is God who will give interpretation to the revelation He gives. Therefore, when we receive a dream, vision, trance, impression, or words, we need to rely on God for the interpretation and diligently seek Him. We are not to make it an interpretive free-for-all. Joseph understood this in regards to dreams and operated accordingly.

> **Genesis 40:8 (NLT)** And they replied, "We both had dreams last night, but there is no one here to tell us what they mean." "Interpreting dreams is God's business," Joseph replied. "Tell me what you saw."

> **Genesis 41:14-16, 25 (NLT)** Pharaoh sent for Joseph at once, and he was brought hastily from the dungeon. After a quick shave and change of clothes, he went in and stood in Pharaoh's presence. "I had a dream last night," Pharaoh told him, "and none of these men can tell me what it means. But I have heard that you can interpret dreams, and that is why I have called for you." "It is beyond my power to do this," Joseph replied. "But God will tell you what it means and will set you at ease.". . ."Both dreams mean the same thing," Joseph told Pharaoh. "God was telling you what He is about to do.

Nebuchadnezzar recognized this about God after Daniel gave an interpretation of his dream as recorded in Daniel chapter two.

> **Daniel 2:47 (NLT)** The king said to Daniel, "Truly, your God is the God of gods, the Lord over kings, a revealer of mysteries, for you have been able to reveal this secret."

Step 1: *Get in the habit of recording God's communication to you.* Whether the communication comes in the form of dreams, visions, words, or impressions; record them. Get in the habit of writing them down. Record it as accurately as possible and give attention to detail. Make notes when God speaks to you. What emotions and feelings did you sense? What were the details of the dream? What were the details of the revelation?

Step 2: *You must remember the bottom-line is this: you simply want to know what God wants you to know.* Don't complicate the process; keep it as simple and straightforward as possible.

Step 3: *Always look for the direct and obvious message first.* The Roman military officer Cornelius received a direct and obvious message from the Lord in a vision. In Acts chapter ten, we read that in this vision an angel approached him. He said in a straightforward manner to send a servant to the town Joppa. There he would find a man named Peter staying with one called Simon the leatherworker who lives near the shore. The servant was to ask this one named Peter to come and visit Cornelius. It doesn't get more direct than that.

Sometimes the Lord speaks that directly to us. *When we do get a direct word, we confirm in prayer whether or not it is as direct as it appears.* When we appropriately test it and find that it is as direct as it appears, we move accordingly.

Step 4: *Discover the clues when interpreting the indirect revelation.* God many times gives us His message shadowed in symbolism. I think God does this to keep us humble, dependent upon Him, and seeking Him out in our lives. Sometimes this forces us to engage other brothers and sisters to help us find interpretation, and we know how much God loves interdependence and community. It also is a catalyst to help us think on the Lord and His kingdom when we meditate on the mystery of God's communication.

To begin this process, it is important to confess our dependence on God and go through the process I earlier described. Make sure you are spiritually prepared and exercise your spiritual authority in binding any demonic influence as you begin the process. Renounce before God any mere human logic, imaginations, or previous experience, which would conflict with God's mind and will. Finally, pray for the Holy Spirit to fill you up, so you can truly understand what God is saying to you.

Second, identify the key components of the revelation and begin to unearth what they symbolize in God's communication to you. Then, work your way through a series of questions.

Question #1: Is there any biblical symbolism in the received revelation? Is there a cloud, or fire, or a dove, or rain, or wind, et cetera? If so, what do these objects communicate in Scripture?

I have had dreams in which wolves occupied the better part of the dream. I know what wolves depict in the Scriptures. I have had dragons in some dreams, and I know what the Scriptures say about dragons. Sometimes when you are searching for an answer, the Lord brings a Scripture to mind; look it up and see what the Lord is trying to reveal to you.

I have had dreams in which a strong wind and fire were components. My wife has had many dreams in which she was living in and around Jerusalem in ancient days, and biblical characters were in the dream. God was communicating to us through the dream on a subject that characterized the biblical characters.

Question #2: Is there contemporary symbolism? What is associated with a certain object today? What does a person or position represent? What is associated with a certain type of vehicle? What can a certain type of activity represent?

I have had many dreams that centered on things

such as futuristic submarines, different types of aircraft like stealth fighter planes, large passenger aircrafts, race cars, et cetera. I have had dreams in which I was interacting with Presidents of countries and world-famous individuals. All of those objects were pieces to a puzzle that symbolized a topic or message God desired to communicate to me.

Question #3: Have you received any other revelation from God that has been similar? If so, how, and what have you discerned God previously saying to you? Or does this revelation contribute to an explanation of what you have previously received? Sometimes I have reoccurring dreams, or dreams with similar elements. Many times reoccurring dreams are communicating confirmation or urgency to something He has previously communicated.

Question #4: Do the Scriptures give us any clues to interpretation? Now when I read my Bible, I look for clues that God has given people in the Scriptures to help them interpret His revelation. One such clue is found in Joseph's interpretation of Pharaoh's dream in Genesis chapter forty-one. Pharaoh had a dream in which there were seven fat cows that were eaten up by seven skinny cows; and then seven plump heads of grain that were eaten up by seven shriveled heads of grain. Joseph interpreted the number seven to represent years. The fat cows and plump heads of grain represented seven years of abundance while the skinny cows and shriveled heads of grain represented seven years of famine that would eat up the abundance of the seven good harvest years. Then he gave an interpretive clue in verse thirty-two.

> **Genesis 41:32 (NLT)** As for having the dream twice, it means that the matter has been decreed by God and that He will make these events happen soon.

Joseph said that Pharaoh having the dream twice meant that God was saying these events would happen soon.

You will find similar clues as you read other Scriptures. I try to remember such clues, and try to apply them as I interpret what God might be saying to me. It is amazing how often I might be wrestling through the meaning of a dream or a word and find symbols in the Scripture that speak directly to interpretation.

Added Help: Enlist others who havc a track record of accurate interpretation of indirect revelation. God does give certain people a greater capacity to interpret dreams, visions, and words given to us by God. All of us are privilege and graced in this discipline, but some are enabled by God in a special way for this task. I want to encourage you to spend time in the interpretation process yourself before you go to others, but do use others. God loves it when His people operate in interdependence and community. Sometimes God does not release an interpretation to us so that we must seek out others in the body of Christ.

Principle #4: "Act on the Words Received with Wisdom."

When Joseph was interpreting the dreams for Pharaoh in Genesis chapter forty-one, he then used wisdom in what to do with the message of the dreams.

> **Genesis 41:33-37 (NLT)** "My suggestion is that you find the wisest man in Egypt and put him in charge of a nationwide program. Let Pharaoh appoint officials over the land, and let them collect one-fifth of all the crops during the seven good years. Have them gather all the food and grain of these good years into the royal storehouses, and store it away so there will be

> food in the cities. That way there will be enough to eat when the seven years of famine come. Otherwise disaster will surely strike the land, and all the people will die." Joseph's suggestions were well received by Pharaoh and his advisers.

God gives us His mind and message to act on it. He might simply speak so that we can strategically, intentionally, and insightfully pray with force and belief. Maybe it is to give us wisdom on how to handle a situation coming up and no one needs to know what was received but us. Maybe there are to be steps of action taken, like our text above with Joseph, and the hundreds of other texts in the Scriptures. Joseph made a suggestion to Pharaoh on what to do with the message the Lord had given. The suggestion included wisdom, it took initiative, it required action, and organization.

We must apply godly, biblical wisdom and apply ourselves to hard work when necessary. God doesn't give us the prophetic as a novelty to play with like a toy. Neither does He make the effort to speak to us so that we ignore Him and go our own way. The prophetic is not for people to live in some ethereal, surreal existence. This many times is why people are scared of the prophetic. It takes people away from functioning in practical, godly wisdom and sends them to "Weirdsville." We cannot throw out Scripture, nor the rest of the spiritual gifts God has given to us. The Scriptures tell us what characterizes wisdom from God.

> **James 3:17 (NASB)** But the wisdom from above is first pure, then peaceable, gentle, reasonable, full of mercy and good fruits, unwavering, without hypocrisy.

Sometimes God really stretches our faith and asks us to step out in a way that might betray conventional wisdom. The Scriptures are filled with such examples (Red Sea, Jericho Walls). When such times come we need to make sure we test such words, double test, even triple test, and then move out in conviction and faith. This happened to us recently.

We were in the process of preparing our church to expand the facilities. We would need approximately $2.5 million to complete the remodel and we had approximately $750,000 on hand. The elders and their spouses were in prayer one afternoon and everyone heard that we were to proceed, for the Lord was not going to bring the rest of the needed funds in until we began building. This was not a very comforting word to me, and I quickly suggested we double-check it, just to make sure! We did, and everyone received that the previous word was correct. That meant talking to the contractor and telling them we would start construction. The only caveat was that they had to trust that over $1.7 million would come in after they started the project. It meant communicating to our church family we would be putting ourselves at risk to the tune of just under two million dollars. I tested what was received with a couple of other leaders who have a great measure of gifting in the prophetic - they all independently received the same answer.

Well, I began the process of meeting with people and presenting to our church family the situation. We are a very blue-collar group of people who gave everything we could when we gave the $750,000. Everywhere I turned, everyone I talked with agreed to proceed. The Lord had said that He would give us the necessary favor needed with everyone, and He did. As I am writing the ending to this book, we are just now finishing up the project and we have witnessed God miraculously provide for every dollar along the way, over $1.5 million in the last one hundred-twenty days.

There is still $370,000 needed to finish off the project, which a man has committed to cover for us.

The bottom line; God gives us words to act on. Keep the three components distinct, and when you have ascertained the application steps God wants you to take - step out!

CHAPTER 11

MINISTERING WITH MANNERS

PRAYING WELL WITH OTHERS

In closing, let me present some etiquette that we need to employ when we are ministering to others in the prophetic. This comes from our experiences of leading a church filled with many people who hear God's voice and have hearts to minister. It is similar to parents who teach their children manners and how to play well with others. These are guidelines we teach and try to employ that make it safe for large numbers of people to move and minister in the prophetic. We do not want to misrepresent the Lord or unnecessarily offend people and thereby discredit this ministry.

ASK PERMISSION

I remember the first time someone came to me with a "word from the Lord." I had no background or frame of reference. They simply came up and told me a "word from the Lord" about a leader in the church. It was an incriminating word, and I was wondering why he felt the liberty to impose it on me. I was taken back and even somewhat offended at his intrusion. He dropped the word on me and took off. What was I to do with the package he left at my doorstep? Several months later I discovered that what he said was true, but since I had no frame of reference for the prophetic, it was of no benefit to me. Before ministering to anyone regarding the prophetic, make sure you ask permission at each step, and make sure they have a frame of reference to be able to handle the word. *Remember, ministering the prophetic is to serve and benefit others, not validate ourselves.* Ask the question, "Is the Lord requiring me to share this disclosure or does He want me to pray and minister in light of what I received?"

DON'T SPEAK TO SENSITIVE SUBJECTS WITHOUT A PROVEN TRACK RECORD

Unless you have much experience with a high accuracy level, don't speak to sensitive subjects. These would be subjects such as marriage, children being born to couples struggling with infertility, money, et cetera. Even if you have experience and a proven track record, when the Lord gives you something regarding a sensitive subject, make sure you are supposed to share it. Remember that you are dealing with people's lives. This is not an experiment with laboratory mice.

Now that I have put those qualifiers in place, let me say that if the Lord does give to you His intentions and will for someone through prayer, and you are certain and have tested that it is of the Lord - then obey the Lord. It could minister greatly to the person.

One illustration of this was a couple that could not have children due to a diagnosed physiological disorder in the mother. To say they were disheartened would be an understatement. She shared her story in tears, so some of us gathered around her to pray a healing prayer as an encouragement to her heart. While we were praying, my wife heard that in one year she would be holding a baby boy in her arms. That was a risky word to share in our friend's emotional moment. Cindy leaned over and told me what she kept receiving and wanted to know what she should do. I quickly prayed while the praying of others was going on and believed that Cindy was to share it. Exactly one year later to the very hour, our friend gave birth to a baby boy. They now have two children! This experience continues to be a source of encouragement to our friends.

PRESENT IN A POSITIVE AND EDIFYING MANNER

Remember that people are to be strengthened and built up. Our objective is restoration and edification. We need to present ourselves and the message we receive to others in humility and love. We need to present in a positive manner as much as possible. Don't present yourself in a manner that looks down, but present in humility and joy. Serve and be a servant, do not think of yourself as a modern day Elijah or John the Baptist speaking to hard-hearted Pharisees.

HAVE INTEGRITY

Don't think or act like everything you say is something you received prophetically. If you observe something with natural senses in the natural world, do not pass it off as if you prophetically received it! Also, distinguish what you received as prophetic and what you are communicating that might be your commentary or wisdom. In fact, as much as possible, if you are able to minister to someone without communicating that you received it prophetically - do so. We tell our people to be "super" natural as much as you can, versus trying to always be "supernatural" in your communication.

BEWARE OF MANIPULATION

People many times are guilty of presenting prophetic words with language that causes a person to feel manipulated and imposed upon. For instance, if you approach someone with the words, "The Lord said. . ." or "This is a message from the Lord for you. . ." or any other similar line, the person you are talking to immediately feels imposed upon. A person less mature in the faith might feel that if they do not receive or act on what you say that God will strike them with lightening or their fate will be the same as that of Ananias and Sapphira.

We train our people to gain permission to give someone any prophetic disclosure they have received and then say, "I have received this in prayer or through a dream, et cetera, test it and see if it rings true as being from the Lord." Then you leave that person's response and action to the word between them and the Lord. You simply are the mail person delivering the message in love, not a law enforcement officer.

IN CLOSING

I trust this little book (by God's grace) was beneficial to you. Let me encourage you to live sensitive to the fact that God speaks to mankind and to you personally! You don't want to be like Samuel and not recognize God's voice. Begin trusting every aspect of your life to the care of the Lord, believing that He delights in every detail of your life. He will lead and guide your every step. Read the scriptures with a renewed sensitivity to the frequency and diverse ways God's spoke to mankind. Enjoy your walk and communication with God at a new level. He loves to communicate with His children! What an awesome privilege!

(Footnotes)

[1] Jack Deere, *Hearing the Voice of God*, (Grand Rapids: Zondervan Publishing House, 1996)

[2]Strong, J. (1996). *Enhanced Strong's Lexicon*. Ontario: Woodside Bible Fellowship.

[3]Wayne Grudem, *Systematic Theology: An Introduction to Biblical Doctrine*, (Grand Rapids: Zondervan Publishing House, 1994), p. 1049

[4]Dale Fredrick Bruner, *A Theology Of The Holy Spirit*, (Eugene: Wipf and Stock Publishers, 1998), p. 142-143

[5]Larry D. Hart, *Truth Aflame; A Balanced Theology for Evangelicals and Charismatics*, (Nashville: Thomas Nelson Publishers, 1999), p. 52

[6]Ibid., [J. Rodman Williams , *Renewal Theology,* Vol. 1 (Grand Rapids: Zondervan Publishers, 1988), p. 44

[7]Wayne Grudem, Systematic Theology: An Introduction to Biblical Doctrine, (Grand Rapids: Zondervan Publishing House, 1994), p. 1016.

[8]Paul Enns, The Moody Handbook Of Theology, (Chicago: Moody Press, 1989), p. 636.

[9]Ray C. Steadman, Body Life, (Glendale: Regal Books, 1972), p. 39.

JESUS MINISTRY
INTERNATIONAL

This book was produced by Jesus Ministry International. We hope it has been helpful to you in living in the freedom Christ Jesus has for you. If you would like to know more about us we invite you to write to:

Jesus Ministry International
P.O. Box 2014
Tacoma, WA 98401

or go to www.jesusministryintl.org